CW00446509

Lincoln's Engineering Industries:
A Concise History, c.1780-1980s

Editor: ANDREW WALKER

Published by
The Survey of Lincoln, 2021

ISBN 978-0-9931263-6-9

ACKNOWLEDGEMENTS

The chapters produced by all of the contributors in this collection have been the result of a significant amount of research, much of which has taken place during a particularly challenging time. I would like to thank all of my 15 fellow authors for their long-term commitment to and enthusiasm for this project.

Very sadly, a number of people involved with this work have not lived to see the final publication. I'd like to pay tribute to their contributions. Hugh Cooke's chapter was largely completed prior to his passing, and I would like to thank Janet Cooke for giving permission for her husband's work to be included here. Chris Lester played a key part in early discussions regarding this work's possible content and his suggestions concerning potential contributors to this volume were extremely helpful. Chris's expertise and enthusiasm for this project, and the city and county's industrial archaeology more generally, were much valued by many of the contributors. Finally, The Survey of Lincoln, and the world of local and regional history more generally, lost a very distinguished figure in 2020 with the passing of Dennis Mills. Since The Survey of Lincoln's inception in 1995, Dennis was always an extremely active participant in its activities and a regular contributor to its publications. Over the years, like many involved in the local history of Lincoln, I have benefited enormously from Dennis's extensive knowledge, enthusiasm and contacts.

I would also like to express my gratitude to several members of The Survey of Lincoln who have provided tremendous support to me in my editorial role, commenting on earlier versions of the text and the content of the map and gazetteer. Thanks particularly to Beryl George, John Herridge, Michael J. Jones, Ken Redmore and Geoff Tann. I am grateful as well to Chris Hewis and the Saxilby History Group for permitting use of historic images from the John Wilson Collection. The Survey of Lincoln is indebted to Anthony D. Hancock, Maurice Hodson, Ray Hooley and John Wilson for ensuring the preservation of visual images relating to Lincoln's industrial past. Their generosity in allowing researchers access to these sources over the years is gratefully acknowledged.

Staff members at Lincolnshire Archives, Lincoln Central Library and the Museum of Lincolnshire Life are thanked for the assistance they have provided to the authors. Another key information source has been the freely-available website and charity, *Grace's Guide to British Industrial History*. I am grateful to all those involved with operating this valuable information resource.

Finally, as a number of contributors note, preserving the industrial history and heritage of the city is an ongoing challenge. The work of all those who have helped preserve it to date needs to be acknowledged.

Andrew Walker
October 2021

Lincoln's Engineering Industry: An Overview

Andrew Walker

Lincoln's significance as an engineering centre is rather understated in the representation of its past, both in the histories written about the city, and in the content of many of its own self-generated profiles as a tourist destination. This volume, produced by The Survey of Lincoln, seeks in part to address this gap. It focuses solely on the city's history as an engineering centre, exploring a diverse range of engineering-related manufacturers, whilst also dedicating particular attention to the 'big four' companies with which Lincoln was particularly associated – Clayton & Shuttleworth, William Foster & Company, Robey & Company, and Ruston, Proctor & Company. In a volume of this size it is of course impossible to provide a comprehensive portrait. However, the aim is to summarise current historical research on these companies, raise new questions to encourage future research and to signpost additional sources where more detailed information can be found.

The authors who have contributed to this collection bring with them a wide range of different experiences that inform their approaches. Some have direct experience of working in the city's engineering companies, including a number who can trace their family links to the founders of some of these concerns. Several have academic interests in the wider history of Lincoln; and others have a particular interest in the way in which the city represents its past, both to local inhabitants and also to those from further afield. At a time when there are particular concerns about the ongoing loss of some of the surviving artefacts associated with the city's engineering past, it seemed an especially timely moment in which to produce such a volume.

Part of the former Clayton & Shuttleworth Stamp End Works at Waterside South, prior to partial demolition of the building shown, which took place between 2015 and 2017. *(Courtesy of SLHA).*

This chapter aims to provide a broad-brush narrative, presenting an overarching, but not comprehensive, history of Lincoln's engineering history, ranging from its origins in earlier trades, such as blacksmithing, up to the present day. It signposts relevant chapters within the work at appropriate moments, where more details can be found about the companies and themes mentioned.

The gazetteer at the end of the publication, together with the extensive bibliography, provides readers with some further leads for more detailed research should they wish to delve deeper into this fascinating and important topic.

Pre-1780: Proto-engineering provision

Lincoln's engagement with engineering has a long history. Those involved in occupations associated with some aspects of metal working for instance, such as blacksmiths, can be traced back to the Romans. Demand for goods produced by such workers began with the need to serve the Roman army in the mid-first century AD. Archaeological research has suggested that immigrant traders and craftspeople played a large role in manufacturing and repairing equipment. The principal industrial areas in the subsequent Roman city were in the suburbs built immediately outside the city's walls, including that to the south of the River Witham where remains of blacksmiths' workshops have been found. A substantial amount of metal working (as well as non-metal manufacture) was undertaken in the Anglo-Scandinavian period in the tenth and eleventh centuries, as exemplified by archaeological excavation evidence at a site on Flaxengate. Subsequently, Lincoln's medieval and early-modern economic life was principally associated with being an ecclesiastical centre, an important hub of the agricultural and woollen trades, and, to a lesser extent, a significant pottery manufacturing base. Other remains have indicated that metal working was also taking place on other sites in the Lower City and Wigford. From wardens' accounts books, it seems that, in 1293 and 1297 there were smiths, shear-grinders, lead-beaters, farriers and goldsmiths working in the city.

Since the medieval period, mills have been a significant feature of the city's townscape. By 1265, a windmill had been erected on the South Common by the canons of neighbouring St Katherine's Priory. Several windmills were operational on the ridge, visible as travellers approached the city from the west. Although not all were in existence simultaneously, at least six were in operation at one time on the cliff edge. John Speed's map of the city of 1610 includes representations of four mills to the north west of the city and three to the north east. According to Francis Hill, in *Medieval Lincoln*, there were also several water mills and horse-powered mills used in the city in 1555 when there was no wind. In order to maintain these mills' mechanisms, engineering skills of some description were evidently needed.

The 1780s to 1850s: The emergence of an engineering industry

According to the surviving records, by the final decades of the eighteenth century, the trades and crafts in which apprentices were employed in Lincoln included bakers, cabinetmakers, carpenters, cordwainers and grocers. Rather less often, ministering to the fashion needs of the day, were makers of perukes (wigs) and mantuas (women's over-gowns). In addition, there were apprentices attached to masters from engineering-related occupations including blacksmiths, boatwrights, whitesmiths, patternmakers and millwrights. A number of long-established millwrights were employing a succession of apprentices by the end of the eighteenth century. John Malam, for instance, who is mentioned in Chris Page's chapter on Lincoln's early engineering firms, was the son of a millwright, and had been apprenticed himself in 1776. Malam had a succession of four different apprentices indentured to him between 1790 and 1797. It is, in part, a result of the supply of such skilled workers in the city that enabled the nascent engineering industry to grow in the city. As Chris Page notes, in addition to millwrights, iron and brass founders had become established in the city by the early nineteenth century. A number of these were situated on the banks of the River Witham, on both Waterside North and South and subsequently close to the railways along watercourses.

The city's navigable waterways, the River Witham and the Fossdyke, were used for the transportation of both raw materials and finished products. Amongst the first companies to become established near to the River Witham, to the east of the city centre, was Clayton & Shuttleworth, which was based at Stamp End from 1842. A little later, situated to its west, Proctor & Burton, a company that was to be energised by the arrival of Joseph Ruston in 1857. Other companies that developed in the vicinity, and which are the subject of later chapters, include Penney & Company, on Broadgate, mentioned in Chris Page's chapter, and Richard Duckering, whose Waterside North works is examined by one of the founder's descendants, Mark Duckering. Robert Robey first began operating a foundry in St Rumbold Street in 1854, before swiftly relocating to larger premises on Canwick Road at the Globe Works. Robey's is explored in a chapter by Adam Cartwright.

The 1850s to 1910s: Sustained growth following the arrival of the railway

The somewhat belated arrival of the railway in Lincoln brought about significant benefits to its early engineering industry. The Midland Railway opened its line from the city to Nottingham in 1846. Two years later, the Great Northern Railway began operating a line linking Lincoln to Boston and Peterborough, and then connecting to the London to York mainline. In 1848-9, the third railway company to reach the city was the Manchester, Sheffield and Lincolnshire Railway (later to become the Great Central Railway), which opened a branch connecting Lincoln to

Hull and Grimsby. Later, three further important railway developments were completed with the opening of a direct route to London, via Grantham, in 1867; then the building of a 'high level' line, with its bridge over the lower High Street, giving access to Sleaford; and finally, of some significance for the burgeoning engineering industry, a largely freight-based line from Chesterfield was opened by the Lancashire, Derbyshire and East Coast Railway in 1897. This brought significant quantities of primary materials, notably coal and iron into Lincoln, feeding its industries' needs. The transport improvements that resulted allowed both raw materials and finished products to be moved in and out of the city speedily and economically.

The Engineer, a periodical, published an article entitled 'A visit to a Lincoln engineering works' on 23 May 1913. It explained the benefits of engineering firms being situated in Lincoln:

> Iron and coal, if not mined on the spot, are obtainable from the neighbouring counties of Derbyshire, Nottinghamshire and Yorkshire. The great industrial markets of the Midlands are close at hand. The immediate neighbourhood absorbs a considerable quantity of agricultural implements and machinery. Facilities for export are … excellent.

With the arrival of the railways, several engineering firms in the city either moved, such as Robey's, and Foster's, or re-orientated their sites, including Clayton & Shuttleworth, to ensure optimum use could be made of the railways in the transportation of the bulky agricultural equipment, which formed the major output of a number of these companies.

The development of Clayton & Shuttleworth is considered in Rob Wheeler's chapter. The company's first portable steam engine was manufactured in 1845. As White's 1856 trade directory noted of the firm, it was Lincoln's largest employer at the time, with 700 men and boys at the works:

> Their steam engines for setting in motion their boulting, threshing, straw shaking, riddling and winnowing machines are on wheeled carriages drawn by horses and they are equal in finish and workmanship to railway locomotives.

The production of agricultural machinery such as portable steam engines, threshing machines and traction engines grew rapidly from the 1850s to the early 1870s, when growth slowed temporarily as a result of the Agricultural Depression. Lincoln's engineering firms increased both in size and number and were principally responsible for driving the demographic growth of the city between 1841 and 1891, from a population of 13,896 to 41,491 respectively. By Joseph Ruston's death in June 1897, the company which partially bore his name had produced some 20,500 steam engines and 10,750 threshing machines, somewhat fewer than the equivalent figures for Clayton & Shuttleworth of 26,000 and 24,000 in 1890. The early years of Ruston, Proctor & Company are considered in Lesley Clarke's chapter.

However, not all of Lincoln's engineering companies thrived during this period. Despite potentially sound product ranges, several engineering businesses over-extended themselves and ran out of capital. This, for instance was the fate of Benjamin Taplin and Joseph Lee's Patent Crank and Traction Engine Works at St Peter at Gowt's, which, as Nicholas Moore explains in his chapter examining the company, only operated between 1861 and 1862 but had a longer-lasting significance.

The railways facilitated not just the transportation of the finished products from the city's factories but also the in-migration of many of its workforce. From the 1850s onwards, workers moved into the city, taking up residence near these works, especially from the 1870s, in the newly-developing terraced streets of the Monks Road and lower High Street districts. Many migrated short distances from the surrounding rural districts within the county, attracted by the steady and relatively well-paid industrial jobs, manufacturing farm machinery that was steadily reducing demand for agricultural labourers. Others, often more skilled and experienced workers, such as iron moulders and turners, moved to Lincoln from nearby counties, such as Nottinghamshire, Derbyshire and Yorkshire.

Long-distant migrant skilled workers were especially prominent amongst the first-wave of workers moving into the city. Particularly conspicuous in the 1851 census were several Cornish-born engineers, blacksmiths, moulders, and especially boiler makers, who were resident in the Waterside and Sincil Street areas. For instance, Hugh Glasson, aged 26, was lodging at 16 Sincil Street in a household headed by his older brother, John, 29. Both John and Hugh were boilermakers and born in Cornwall. Sincil Street was also home in 1851 to Richard Eddy, 25, a boilermaker from Cornwall, who, it is highly likely, was related to 22-year-old William Eddy, similarly occupied, also born in Cornwall, living at Hewson's Court, Waterside South. Brothers Richard, 27, and Lewis Trevorrow, 25, a blacksmith and boilermaker respectively, lodged at 43 Waterside South. They were both born in Hayle, Cornwall, as was George Kellway, 21, a boilermaker, listed as a visitor at neighbouring 39 Waterside South. By 1861, Kellway was married to Lincolnshire-born Charlotte, with five young children and living in St Swithin's parish. It is probable that Lincoln's expanding engineering firms were recruiting well-trained, ambitious young employees from established companies such as Harvey & Company, based in Hayle, Cornwall, which not only served the south-west county's copper and tin mines and smelting works, but also had an international reputation for its steam-powered beam engines.

Lincoln's agricultural engineering production grew steadily from the 1850s to the 1880s, satisfying the needs of not just a British market, but an international one. In Europe, substantial business was undertaken in the extensive cereal-growing lands of Austro-Hungary and, after the Crimean War, in Russia. By the end of the nineteenth century all of Lincoln's 'big four' companies had branches in Budapest and several other eastern European cities. Beyond Europe, these engineering companies were also transacting significant business in South America and Australasia. According to the company's records, between 1909 and 1913, of 408 threshing machines delivered by William Foster & Company, 247 were exported, chiefly to Buenos Aires. The North American prairies also became home to much Lincoln-manufactured engineering machinery by the end of the nineteenth century. The number of employees at Clayton & Shuttleworth's Lincoln works grew from 520 in 1854 to 2300 in 1885; Ruston, Proctor & Company employed 700 in 1870 and this had grown to 1600 by 1889; and Robey's employed 503 men and boys in 1871 and had 1200 employees in 1890. In the 1901 census, Lincoln recorded 5543 males over the age of 10 years who were occupied in 'trades associated with metals, machines, implements and conveyances', constituting 35% of the city's male workforce.

This growth in trade and manufacturing necessitated much physical expansion of the city's engineering works in the later part of the nineteenth century. A good proportion of this growth took place immediately to the south-west of the city centre, in an area which, by 1885, was called New Boultham. Here, initially, were located the substantial woodworking divisions of both Ruston's, at its Anchor Road works (from 1865) and later Foster's (from 1883). From the mid-1880s, much working-class residential development took place in this newly-named district – formerly the site of Derby Farm, known as Derby Grounds – though from the outset there were concerns relating to the area's low-lying nature and the inadequacy of sanitary arrangements. Further industrial development in New Boultham by both Ruston's and Foster's followed. Ruston's constructed a Boiler Works, its Boultham Works, and then the Spike Island Works on Beevor Street in 1915. Foster's relocated its entire operations from its old Wellington Works home on Waterside North, which was sold in 1900 to Rainforth's, examined in a chapter by Adam Cartwright, and constructed an entirely new complex beside its woodworking department, which it called the New Wellington Works. The name acknowledged the late William Foster's admiration of the Duke of Wellington, whose nickname, appropriately, was the Iron Duke. The fortunes of William Foster & Company are explored in a later chapter in this volume.

Whilst Foster's and Ruston's began to colonise New Boutham, Robey's confined itself principally to its existing site to the east of Canwick Road, and Clayton & Shuttleworth was able to extend its works eastwards on land adjacent to its existing Stamp End property on

Waterside South, building an electricity power station on Spa Road, the Titanic Works, the Tower Works and Abbey Works between 1912 and 1916.

By the turn of the twentieth century, Lincoln's major engineering companies were attempting to diversify their product ranges, moving away from solely agricultural engineering. To an extent, this was prompted by the Agricultural Depression in Britain from the 1870s to the 1890s, caused by the collapse of grain prices following the opening up of the North American market by transport developments. Ruston's began producing steam rollers, traction engines, locomotives and mechanical excavators in the last three decades of the nineteenth century. As Lesley Clarke notes in her chapter, Ruston's 'steam navvy' excavation equipment was used extensively in the digging of the Manchester Ship Canal in 1887. In the 1890s, Robey's began targeting extractive and industrial markets through the production of mining engines, dynamos and gas and oil engines. Foster's saw the growth of road transport as a potential market, but focussed on an old motive power source, in its development of steam road vehicles in 1904.

The 1910s to 1940s: Significant challenges and threats

The years immediately before the outbreak of the First World War proved challenging for Lincoln's engineering companies, and indeed for much of British industry. In Spring 1911, it seemed, superficially at least, that many of the city's larger engineering firms were prospering, with Clayton & Shuttleworth reporting a profitable year's trading allowing shareholders to be rewarded with a 5% dividend, and Ruston, Proctor & Company recording an annual profit of £66,024. However, with prices rising sharply from 1907 onwards, workers' wages in real terms were falling significantly. This led to a substantial amount of strike action across Britain as trade unions sought to obtain wage increases for their members. In July 1911, the *Lincolnshire Chronicle* reported that, as a result of a boilermakers' strike, over 1000 men had ceased work in Lincoln. By August 1911, the city's police were compelled to intervene to protect strike breakers. This industrial unrest was the background against which riotous activity took place in the city in the unprecedented heat of 18 and 19 August 1911, sparked by a national railway strike. This industrial dispute significantly disrupted the flow of raw materials and finished products to and from the engineering works.

During the First World War, Lincoln's engineering industry responded swiftly to the changing needs of a wartime economy and society, facilitated by the direct intervention of government, co-ordinating contracts and the supply of raw materials. The city's firms manufactured armaments, military vehicles, and aeroplanes, such as the Sopwith Camel, produced by Ruston's, and the Vickers Vimy bomber at Clayton & Shuttleworth's. New factory buildings were swiftly erected to accommodate the wartime manufacturing needs, with Ruston's erecting new structures on the banks of the River Witham at New Boultham, and Spike Island. During the war, Clayton & Shuttleworth built the Abbey Works and Clayton Forge in which, amongst other products, railway wagons were manufactured, both for use in Britain and in Europe. The eastern end of the West Common became a dedicated testing and acceptance site for many aircraft manufactured in the city, with a runway and hangars being erected there.

By the end of the war, Ruston's alone had produced over 2000 aircraft, manufacturing more Sopwith Camels than any other company. Charles Parker's chapter examines the city's wartime aircraft production in more detail. Perhaps Lincoln's best-known contribution to wartime manufacture was the development at William Foster's, under the leadership of William Tritton, of the tank, first produced in 1916.

The switch to military production saw a radical change in the personnel employed at the city's engineering works, with the hiring of a sizeable female workforce, in large part to replace many of the factories' male employees who had responded to the call to fight for their country. Scrutiny of Lincoln's building plans for the war years reveal that many of the city's engineering firms, besides expanding their production facilities, were also, from 1916, hastily erecting toilets for their newly-recruited female workers. In order to accommodate the substantial numbers of workers needed to maintain wartime production, many of the city's large companies bought up housing stock in the city, and rooms were rented out to their employees.

Following the end of the war, the city's engineering companies returned swiftly to a peacetime footing. This meant the speedy withdrawal from the workforce of women and their replacement by men returning from military service. Following a short-term post-war boom, however, the engineering companies then suffered a protracted economic decline, caused by a global depression. Lincoln's industry was disproportionately affected as a consequence of the export-orientated nature of much of its companies' businesses, and its competitiveness in overseas markets was hampered

A Ruston oil engine about to leave Beevor Street en route to the newly-opened Sound City film studios at Shepperton, transported by a Pickford's Cammell-hauled low-loader, c. 1931. (*Image courtesy of the John Wilson Collection, Saxilby History Group*).

considerably by the government's decision, encouraged by the Chancellor of the Exchequer, Winston Churchill, to strengthen the pound by returning it to the Gold Standard in 1925. The reduction in demand for many of Lincoln's steam-powered products was compounded by the move away from steam-powered technology to the mainly diesel – and petrol-fuelled internal combustion engine.

In the case of Clayton & Shuttleworth, its involvement in pre-war Russia proved particularly burdensome following the success of the revolutionary forces that did not honour commitments made by their predecessors. Clayton & Shuttleworth, though, were not alone in their dependence on Russian business. According to Board of Trade figures, 29.6% of all UK agricultural machinery exports in 1913 were to Russia. The second largest export market for such goods at that time was Germany, with 8.0%. However, the Russian difficulties did not constitute the principal reason for Clayton & Shuttleworth's subsequent demise, as Rob Wheeler makes clear in his chapter. The company was reorganised, with Clayton Wagons, formed in 1920, occupying the Titanic Works, Abbey Works and the Clayton Forge, where steam motor wagons and railway stock, amongst other products, were built. Clayton & Shuttleworth continued to manufacture agricultural engineering products from its Stamp End works, but was finally wound up in 1936. Clayton Wagons sold its forge to Coventry-based Thomas Smith's Stamping Works in 1929, when it became Smith-Clayton Forge; the Titanic Works was bought by Clayton-Dewandre, where motor engineering and servo-brake manufacturing took place from 1928 onwards; and a large multi-national American boiler-making company, Babcock and Wilcox, with a long-established Scottish base, purchased the Stamp End Works in 1924. In reporting positively on this latter news, the *Lincolnshire Echo* on 26 April 1924 noted that hundreds of skilled workers in the city had been unemployed for over three years, and that the volume of Clayton & Shuttleworth's 'standard trade' was just 6 per cent of its pre-war levels.

By 1922, according to Board of Trade figures, the value of exports from the United Kingdom of agricultural machinery stood at just 12.7% of the figure in 1913 in real terms. Unemployment in the city rose to 6600 in 1922. The number of insured unemployed workers fell to 1000 in 1927-8, but increased again to 7800 in 1933, over one third of the city's 22,780 insured workpeople at the time. Through much of the interwar period, unemployment in Lincoln remained stubbornly high. As the *Lincolnshire Echo* noted in an editorial on 18 November 1931, in which it supported attempts to introduce new light industries to the city, the unemployment problem in the city was:

> largely due to the fact that we have nearly all our eggs in one basket – engineering. When engineering prospers, Lincoln prospers; when engineering droops the whole city suffers.

Various attempts were made to provide job creation schemes for these often highly-skilled unemployed workers, including the rebuilding of Bracebridge Gas Works in 1932-33. Lincoln's Marks and Spencer, built in 1931, drew upon the labour of some of the city's unemployed workers during its construction. Part of the former site of Harrison's Malleable Iron Works was opened in 1932 to allow the unemployed to maintain their skills. Another small initiative was set up, encouraging the acquisition of a new skill, by teaching some of the unemployed how to drive. In August 1935 it was reported that Lincoln's People's Service Club had bought a car for the purpose, grounds were lent by Ruston & Hornsby, near its woodworking operations, and students from the Bishop's Hostel, on Wordsworth Street, acted as instructors.

In response to the substantial downturn in trade, Ruston, Proctor & Company sought to diversify, moving away from agriculture, and producing oil engines and locomotives. In 1918, the company merged with a smaller enterprise, Richard Hornsby of Grantham, manufacturers of threshing machines and other farm machinery. The new company was named Ruston & Hornsby. The early twentieth-century history of Ruston's is examined in a chapter by Abigail Hunt. In 1919, Ruston's transferred the majority of its agricultural interests to Ransome's of Ipswich, and began to build high-quality cars in its Lincoln-based motor works. Although the cars developed a very good reputation for their quality, only a few were sold. The company also began to build furniture in its New Boultham woodworking facilities which had been expanded significantly during the war. In 1930, the company partnered Bucyrus-Erie, an American company, with which it produced mechanical excavators. Some significant investment was made by the new company, with three new workshops built in 1930 on Beevor Street and a separate administration block constructed in 1931. The history of this company – separate from Ruston & Hornsby – is explored in a chapter by Derek Broughton, who was a former employee of the company.

As with a number of other engineering companies, Foster's was relatively slow to respond to changing technological developments. It was still producing traction engines until 1942. The company acquired Gwynne's Engineering Company in 1927, and, through a newly-established company, Gwynne's Pumps, which was based in Lincoln, the company moved away from farm-related equipment, making hydraulic drainage pumps, used mainly in mines, sewers and upon fenlands. According to the Chairman's annual report, by 1940, Foster's agricultural machinery only comprised 5% of the company's turnover.

As Adam Cartwright's chapter notes, Robey's struggled on during the inter-war years, going into temporary receivership in 1932. However, through various amalgamations, the company continued to operate during this period.

Whilst Lincoln's 'big four' companies found the inter-war years particularly challenging, some of the smaller, nimbler, engineering companies within the city were able to focus upon the development of product ranges that continued to attract markets. The Gowt's Bridge Works of J.T.B. Porter, considered in a chapter by Nicholas Moore, continued to produce high-quality iron work and also branched into gas engineering. Duckering's, another ironwork manufacturer, still made various types of street furniture as well as agricultural machinery, but also began to specialise in kitchen ranges. The Lindum Plough Works of John Cooke, examined in a chapter by his descendant, Hugh Cooke, continued manufacturing farm implements and agricultural vehicles until 1937, when it closed. Edward Clarke's business, which was first opened on Hungate in 1859, later moved to Coultham Street (now Kesteven Street) where it specialised in the production of crankshafts. Clarke's Crank & Forge Company Limited, which is considered later in this work, continued operating in Lincoln throughout this period, for a time becoming part of a combine of companies, the Agricultural & General Engineers, between 1920 and 1932. On Monks Road, William Rainforth & Co. remained in business, focussing particularly upon the manufacture of corn screens. Harrison's Lincoln Malleable Iron Works, explored in Ken Redmore's chapter, moved from its city centre base to more extensive premises in North Hykeham. Like a number of other Lincoln engineering companies, control of Harrison's development moved outside the city as its ownership passed to Ley's Malleable Castings of Derby.

As the re-armament process began in the later 1930s, those companies which had survived began to see a rise in demand for some of their products. According to correspondents writing to the *Lincolnshire Echo* in August 1938, though, military contracts assigned to Lincoln-based firms seemed to be slower arriving than in other cities, such as Birmingham. The onset of war in 1939 ensured that demand rose speedily and extensively. Matilda tanks and armoured tractors were produced by Ruston & Hornsby. The city also manufactured mines, searchlights, Bofors guns and various types of crankshaft for military production. Unlike the First World War, there was a significant amount of continuity, however, between peacetime and wartime production in the city's engineering companies, with thousands of Ruston & Hornsby diesel engines being produced for use in a wide array of military contexts. For instance, they provided power for minesweepers, and refrigeration plants in the Sahara, and for Winston Churchill's underground bunker. During the Second World War, the Germans' French military headquarters, based just outside Paris, was also powered by Lincoln-built Ruston engines.

The 1940s to the present: Responding to technological change and increasing specialisation

Following the Second World War, a further period of reorientation was necessary. Women were once again relieved of their jobs on the engineering works' factory floor. Their employment opportunities were, however, greater than following the First World War, with many female employees working in the administrative departments of the city's engineering companies. By the later twentieth century onwards, opportunities for female engineers in Lincoln's industrial sector were growing, though numbers remain relatively low across the sector. According to an *Engineering UK Report* in 2018, 11% of the UK engineering workforce was female, with just 5% of registered engineers and technicians being women. The UK continues to have the lowest percentage of female engineering professionals in Europe.

Lincoln's major engineering firms began to seek out rather more niche markets. Ruston & Hornsby, for instance, started to develop several types of gas turbines and, in 1952, full-scale production of these began, and they soon became a very significant aspect of the company's operations. Substantial investment had taken place, with the opening of a large new foundry by the company on Beevor Street. The company became one of Europe's leading suppliers of gas turbines in the 1960s.

In 1966, Ruston & Hornsby was bought by English Electric, which, in turn, was purchased by the British industrial conglomerate, General Electric Company (GEC) in 1968. A year later, the Lincoln-based operation became known as Ruston Gas Turbines. In 1989, GEC merged with the heavy-engineering division of the French firm Alsthom, changing its name to Alstom in 1998. By then, the Lincoln subsidiary was known as European Gas Turbines. In 2003, Alstom sold its gas turbines interests, including the Lincoln-based operations, to Siemens, a

multinational company which has operated in the United Kingdom since 1843. Gas turbines continue to be designed and made by the company in Lincoln, with some production still taking place at its city-centre works.

Ruston's Boultham Works, where First World War aircraft and, later, cars were manufactured. The building was demolished in 2019. *(Courtesy of SLHA).*

Derek Broughton's chapter details the fate of Ruston Bucyrus, which continued to produce cranes and excavating equipment in the years following the Second World War. As Derek's chapter indicates, however, a failure to invest significantly in new technological developments seriously undermined the company's competitiveness, leading to a protracted demise. The last machine built in Lincoln left the premises in 2001.

In the years following the Second World War, Robey's principal manufacturing interests were in boilers and winders. However, the company was able to apply its expertise to specialised products as well, such as the manufacture of parts for the Jodrell Bank telescope, including the dish-tilting mechanism, and the roller bearings used in the operation of the telescope, which was opened in 1957.

In 1985, Robey's was acquired by Babcock International, the successor to Babcock and Wilcox, which had bought Clayton & Shuttleworth's Stamp End works in 1924. This company merged with FKI Electricals of Loughborough. A restructuring programme was then undertaken, which included the closure of the Robey's site in 1988.

William Foster & Company and its partner, Gwynne's Pumps were acquired in 1961 by W.H. Allen, Sons & Company, a long-established engineering company originating in Bedford in 1880. Seven years after the acquisition of Foster's and Gwynne's, W.H. Allen became the subject of a merger. The Wellington Foundry closed in 1968, but was then occupied by Ruston Bucyrus and Ruston Gas Turbines until demolition took place in 1983-84.

Whilst a number of Lincoln's longer-established engineering names disappeared from the city in the later decades of the twentieth century, some other engineering provision continued to develop. As Colin Smith's chapter indicates, electronic component manufacturing started in Lincoln in 1958 and had grown significantly by 1981. In that year, Marconi Electronic Devices (MEDL), one of the companies in the GEC organisation, was established with its main base on Carholme Road in Lincoln. Although that has since closed, and is now the location of an extensive residential estate, the company still has a substantial presence on a site in the southern part of the city, on Doddington Road.

Lincoln's reputation as an engineering centre continues. The city's major employer, Siemens, has a workforce based on various sites across the city and its immediate surroundings of more than 1500 people. Between 2010 and 2020 it has invested £48.5m at its Teal Park gas turbine centre and £43.5m at the Ruston site on Waterside South. The company has developed a significant partnership with the University of Lincoln and its School of Engineering.

Seeking information about Lincoln's engineering past is, as several contributors to this collection have suggested, something of a challenge. Arthur Ward's chapter explores some of the remaining physical evidence for the output of the engineering industries, focussing especially upon some of the surviving street furniture manufactured by Lincoln companies. Heather Hughes and Tom Kitchen examine the ways in which Lincoln's engineering past is currently remembered and celebrated through, for instance, memorials relating both to companies, products and individuals. Heather and Tom also provide some information regarding archival and other documentary deposits that relate to the city's engineering past. Throughout the collection, authors have sought to emphasise where buildings and structures relating to their subjects can still be seen. In a number of cases, such as Charles Parker's chapter on the city's aircraft production during the First World War, reference is made to buildings that have recently been demolished.

At a time when STEM subjects (science, technology, engineering and mathematics) are being prioritised in compulsory, further and higher education provision by the government, it seems particularly appropriate to be drawing attention to the engineering-related history of Lincoln. It is to be hoped that the city's longstanding association with this important, and perhaps undervalued, industrial sector will continue to flourish and that rather more attention will be paid in future to celebrating its rich and distinguished past in the city.

Some of Lincoln's Early Engineering Businesses and Iron Foundries

Chris Page

Agriculture has been the dominant industry in Lincolnshire for centuries, supported by craftspeople producing the tools and implements required for use on the land. Craft-based occupations such as wheelwrights, blacksmiths, wire workers, whitesmiths and millwrights supplied such equipment but, by the late eighteenth century, specialist implement makers had appeared. Lincoln then saw a growth in occupations associated with producing a widening range of agricultural equipment.

By 1793, the machine maker Thomas Sawdon was working in Swanpool Court, Lincoln. He had gained a reputation for his corn-dressing and winnowing machines, but it was with his chaff cutter that he became well known. He patented this machine in 1802 and it remained in production until well after his death in 1846. Sawdon's chaff cutter continued to be produced by two other Lincoln manufacturers for many years. They both exhibited examples of this machine at the Royal Agricultural Society of England's show at Lincoln in 1854. Sawdon passed on his business in 1834 to Charles Revill, another machine maker. Revill and his sons continued to produce a similar range of equipment until 1914.

Thomas Sawdon also produced a turnip cutter in 1819, which, he implied, had been given a patent. This brought him into fierce rivalry with Thomas Barrett, another city machine maker. Barrett was in business by the 1790s with a workshop in St Mary's Street and was producing a similar range of products to Sawdon. Barrett was jealous of his rival's 'patent' boast and declared in the newspapers that no one had a patent for a turnip cutter. Thomas Barrett died in 1820, but the business survived, led by his widow, Lucy, and assisted, in the first instance, by three of her sons. Although the business ceased in Lincoln in 1838, on the death of Thomas's son, Robert Barrett, the St Mary's Street works continued under the auspices of Henry Walker. The Barrett family's interests in machine making continued elsewhere in the county, particularly in Boston, where family members had been involved in the industry since at least 1816. Descendants remain in business to this day as W. S. Barrett and Son, making agricultural and horticultural wire-work products and are one of the oldest machine-making businesses in Lincolnshire.

Although winnowing and blowing machines for cleaning corn were some of the primary implements being produced in Lincoln at the start of the nineteenth century, the range of products was beginning to grow. These included linseed cake breakers, chaff cutters and turnip cutters for feeding stock, bean mills, screens and riddles for sieving soil, as well as domestic goods. Makers such as the Dixon family of Unity Square and Henry Walker, who took over the premises of Robert Barrett in 1838, continued to produce winnowing machines and other barn machines. The wire worker William Mitton took over his father's business in 1842 and

Mitton, Penney & Company's rotary corn separator, as advertised in Morris's *Commercial Directory of Lincolnshire*, 1863. (*Chris Page Collection*).

set up the City Wire Works on The Strait, gaining a reputation for his rotary seed cleaner, which he later patented in 1860. Like many small engineering firms, Mitton lacked the financial ability to sustain his business. This was solved when John Penney became a partner. Penney soon took over the business, forming John Penney & Co., with Mitton's seed cleaner being one of its main products. This firm eventually became Penney & Porter Ltd and continued producing seed cleaners, based on Mitton's design, until they closed in 1968.

John Tye senior was born in Branston in 1801. He had established a millwright workshop in Hungate by 1829. His business was that of a typical millwright, building mills, and selling mill stones and ancillary equipment. He and his wife, Sarah, had nine children, one being John Tye junior, born in 1829. John junior took over the business in 1853 and moved the workshop to St Mark's Lane where he built up a significant business manufacturing portable and fixed corn mills to customers across the world. In 1870 Tye went bankrupt, a fate experienced by many early manufacturers.

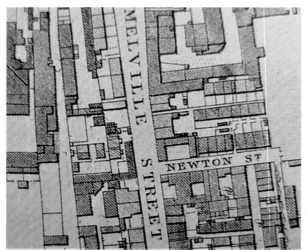

The factory, established in 1865 by Mitton & Co. with William Rainforth, is situated on the northern side of the junction between Melville Street and Newton Street, as shown on Padley's map of 1868. (*Source: Mills Dennis and Wheeler, Robert C., eds, Historic Town Plans of Lincoln, 1610-1920, published for The Lincoln Record Society and The Survey of Lincoln by Boydell and Brewer, Woodbridge, 2004*).

The first iron foundries in Lincoln were on Broadgate and east of Thornbridge, on Waterside South. The millwright John Malam was operating a foundry on Waterside South by 1808. That was the year he died and his widow, Rebecca, and son Joseph Malam continued the business, announcing that they could supply brass and iron castings to any model. By 1815 Joseph was working with his stepfather of six years, a joiner, William Mumby, to make threshing machines at their Waterside South premises but they too had become bankrupt by 1820. The exact location of Joseph Malam and William Mumby's premises is unknown.

John Key had opened his millwright workshops on Broadgate by 1815. He first concentrated on general mill work but soon moved into constructing agricultural machines such as seed drills, turnip cutters and threshing machines. On 3 April 1835, he announced that he had installed a foundry. The firm continued until the death of John Key junior in 1845 when the business was bought by Michael Penistan. In 1855 Penistan moved the workshops and foundry to St Rumbold's Lane. Another foundry was that operated by John Barnby (Barniby or Bernby) which was situated in St Swithin's Parish, at an unknown location. He was an ironfounder operating in 1808 when he buried one of his infant sons. John and his wife Mary were again recorded in 1810 with the birth of another son, after which nothing is known.

It is likely that the foundry occupied by John Barnby was the one that passed into the ownership of the Nottingham iron and brass founder, Thomas Copeland, by 1812. Copeland named it 'The Phoenix Foundry' where he was making a wide variety of machinery for water and windmills, thrashing machines, cranes, ovens, kitchen ranges, bedsteads, brewing pans, pumps and pipes. He also made steam engine boilers, firebars and chains. This business did not last long as he was declared bankrupt in July 1814. The following month, the site was put up for sale. It included a newly-built house, a warehouse, stables and also 'a spacious and substantial building lately used as an iron foundry' with a one-acre paddock behind. A two-day auction in September disposed of his stock in hand and his household furniture. The stock included ovens, grates, palisading, iron bedsteads, malt rollers, bean mills as well as bellows, a cupola and a large quantity of patterns.

James Chambers was the next occupant of this iron foundry. He announced that he had recently taken over Copeland's foundry in an advertisement published in January 1821. Products included 'new and ornamental' stove grates, some with bronze facings and bright steel ornaments, also hot-air stoves for large houses, churches and libraries. Later advertisements showed that he was making many of the standard items such as pipes, grates and parts for agricultural machinery. In 1823, he introduced an improved treadmill for prisons and workhouses, which he priced at between £50 and £100. One of his treadmills was installed at Folkingham Prison in 1825. In that year he erected a bone mill east of the foundry, using an 8-horse-power steam engine by Boulton and Watt. This mill and engine could not have operated for long as they were sold in April 1828. Chambers was producing a wide range of agricultural machinery by 1829, including horse wheels for threshing machines, land pressers and corn drills. His foundry was still busy in August 1831 when a thunderstorm destroyed part of the foundry's tall chimney, injuring some workmen.

This foundry was next taken over by John Burton, in 1835. Burton came from a family of blacksmiths at South Leverton in Nottinghamshire. He ran the foundry on his own, but was later joined by his brother, Theophilus, who was a blacksmith. By 1840 John had gone into partnership with another millwright, James Toyne Proctor, but in 1842 John died. Theophilus took John's place as a partner with Proctor and they were later joined by a young Joseph Ruston. Theophilus left the firm in July 1857, and the firm of Ruston and Proctor was born. The history of Ruston's is examined in subsequent chapters by Lesley Clarke, Abigail Hunt and Derek Broughton.

This chapter merely touches on some of the Lincoln-based craftspeople, millwrights and engineers of the late eighteenth and early nineteenth century. They created a strong engineering legacy in the city, turning rural Lincoln into a major manufacturing centre which produced agricultural and power machinery. These products were distributed throughout the British Isles and across the world.

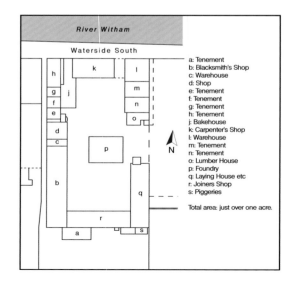

Plan of James Chambers' iron foundry, Waterside South, c.1830. (*Chris Page and Dave Watt*).

THE RISE AND FALL OF CLAYTON & SHUTTLEWORTH

Rob Wheeler

Nathaniel Clayton and Joseph Shuttleworth formed a partnership as iron founders in 1842, based at Stamp End where the latter operated a boatyard. Clayton was in business running a steam packet between Lincoln and Boston but had been trained, perhaps as an apprentice, at the Butterley Iron Works in Derbyshire. The two men believed that the arrival of the railways would ruin trade on the River Witham but that railway construction would offer lucrative business of a general sort for an iron foundry.

They were right on the first count, wrong on the second: the big railway contractors already had a wide network of suppliers and the Great Northern even set up its own foundry in Lincoln rather than rely on local suppliers of unknown quality. The partners aimed to compete for the more technically demanding jobs: a large order for cast-iron water pipes from the Boston Water Company was remembered as one of their early achievements. The cast-iron components for the railway bridge across the River Trent at Radcliffe, opened in 1850, can still be seen; it may be significant that cast-iron pipes and bridges had been among the most advanced products of the Butterley company.

Like most ambitious iron founders at this date, they aspired to produce portable steam engines that could drive agricultural machinery such as threshing drums, and Clayton & Shuttleworth produced their first in 1845. The problem with such engines was that they needed to be light enough for four horses to move them on poor roads; having a solid chassis, an efficient boiler and a sufficiently powerful engine seemed incompatible with this weight limit.

In 1847, T.M. Keyworth and Charles Seely joined the partnership; there are suggestions that Clayton and Shuttleworth were desperate for money. Keyworth was the most respected of the Lincoln merchants; Seely was outstanding as an entrepreneur. The two were already in partnership running Lincoln's newest (and highly profitable) steam mill. Because all partners had unlimited personal liability for the partnership's debts, Clayton, Shuttleworth & Co (which was the new partnership's trading name) was now seen as absolutely safe.

Why should Keyworth and Seely have committed their fortunes to a struggling iron-foundry? The answer seems to lie with a man called Richard Bach, who had been a partner in a Birmingham engineering firm. That partnership was dissolved in 1848 and he moved to Lincoln some time about then. He was something of an inventor and he seems to have realised that it was possible to solve the weight problem by giving a portable engine a sturdy multi-tube boiler and dispensing with a chassis: everything was attached to the boiler. That violated a number of good design principles but it seemed to work: it made it possible to produce an engine of adequate power that did not spew sparks all over a rick yard and which did not tear its boiler apart either. The first engine to his design was made by Clayton, Shuttleworth & Co in October 1848. We do not know the terms of the agreement with Bach; but the partners – and perhaps Seely in particular – realised that there was nothing patentable in this design. Once it became public, every iron foundry in the country would be able to turn them out.

That was where Keyworth and Seely's business skills came in. When the new engine was displayed at the Royal Agricultural Show in 1849, it was offered with all the necessary ancillary machines, notably a portable threshing machine, using a technology fairly standard in corn-milling but of which Natty Clayton and Joe Shuttleworth would have known very little. By this date also, the firm was geared up to produce this range in quantity. In the event, they made 65 engines in 1850, 126 in 1851, and 209 in 1852. They never looked back. Economies of scale meant that production was highly profitable.

Keyworth seems to have looked after the export business. We know he represented the firm at the 1855 Paris Exhibition. He was probably at the Vienna Exhibition of 1857, and recognised that Austria-Hungary offered an enormous export market, with large amounts of grain produced in the south-eastern part of that empire on big estates owned by members of the nobility, who had the capital to invest in new technology and could supply the organisational skills that would ensure it was properly used. Branch establishments were set up in Vienna and in Pest, which assembled engines that had been built in Lincoln and knocked down for ease of transport. These establishments also manufactured a range of agricultural implements, developing local skills and introducing technical advances from western Europe to an agricultural sector that had been somewhat backward.

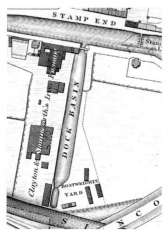

Bach's reward had been an appointment as the firm's salaried engineer. He left in 1852 to return to Birmingham, where he established a firm producing steam engines and boilers, flour mills and circular-saw benches. The last two products sound very similar to ones in the Clayton, Shuttleworth range and may have been products he designed while at Lincoln. He was replaced by William Waller, who introduced a type of engine in which the

Clayton & Shuttleworth's iron foundry from Padley's plan of Lincoln of 1851. The Shuttleworth boatyard on the far side of the dock is still shown.(*Source: Mills Dennis and Wheeler, Robert C., eds, Historic Town Plans of Lincoln, 1610-1920, published for The Lincoln Record Society and The Survey of Lincoln by Boydell and Brewer, Woodbridge, 2004*).

cylinder was placed in an upper extension to the smokebox in order to reduce condensation and improve efficiency. Waller left in 1857. That two engineers should leave after only a few years, and that one should use his designs to set up in competition, seem to have caused the partners to take the view that professional engineers were more trouble than they were worth. It was quite unusual for agricultural-engineering firms to employ such professionals: normally development was an activity carried out by the partners, backed up by a good chief draughtsman, and Clayton, Shuttleworth & Co reverted to this pattern. This attitude that only partners (and their families) could be trusted seems to have extended further. The dispersed Austro-Hungarian operation needed quite a few local managers. George Blakey, who became the managing director in Vienna, was Natty Clayton's wife's nephew; while two of the subjects of the empire who rose to senior positions were married to Shuttleworth relatives.

T.M. Keyworth died in 1858 and that is the point at which the firm lost its edge. Keyworth's sons became partners in his stead, and one of them seems to have been a good linguist who was active in Vienna, but the young Keyworths lacked their father's ability to sense when something was going to fail and were more of a liability than an asset. Charles Seely's interests moved away from Lincoln; the founding partners felt that he was taking his share of the profits without contributing anything, there was a flaming row, and he was bought out.

Natty Clayton and Joe Shuttleworth became wealthy men. The former took to yachting and in 1861 he bought a country villa on the Isle of Wight. Shuttleworth, by then a widower, married into one of the leading gentry families and built Hartsholme Hall as a suitably grand residence. They were certainly interested in improving their products, as is shown by the patents granted, but they had ceased to dream about breakthroughs like that initial creation of the viable portable steam engine.

Consequently, after 1858 there were no real innovations at Stamp End. The firm would note innovations made elsewhere and copy them if they seemed worthwhile. Thus, portable engines were replaced by traction engines, able to move themselves and their associated threshing machine from farm to farm. Replacing wheels by rollers turned a traction engine into a steam roller. The firm maintained a good drawing office, so all these things could be done competently, and their reputation for quality of manufacture was never lost, but slowness to innovate tended to result in their not obtaining the sort of market share which had made portable-engine production so very profitable. For example, by the end of the century they produced a range of heavy-oil engines (or Diesel engines, to use modern terminology) but, so far as one can judge from correspondence with their foreign sales agents, there were numerous variants all selling in fairly small numbers.

Joe Shuttleworth died in 1883, Natty Clayton in 1890, after which Shuttleworth's son

The first portable engine delivered to Hungary by Clayton & Shuttleworth. It was used until 1900. (*Eva Moore*).

Alfred was sole proprietor until 1901 when he made the firm a limited company. Alfred Shuttleworth was a kind-hearted man and a great benefactor to Lincoln but he was not possessed of great business acumen and foresight. Nor did the directors appointed in 1901 seem to bring much, although a new focus on the technical education of the employees was doubtless beneficial.

Meanwhile the whole agricultural-engineering industry was facing two problems. The first was market saturation. The UK market for threshing sets had long been a mature one; replacements were needed from time to time but these products were built to last. By 1900, even the remoter parts of Romania were reaching saturation. The future for expansion was seen as Russia; George Blakey in Vienna had brought his sons up on that basis – presumably learning Russian from an early age. The second problem was competition. The major European countries had their own engineering industries, often pressing their governments for protection from foreign competition; and the burgeoning US industry was seeking inroads into markets like South America that had long been seen as a British preserve. These pressures meant that the business was less profitable than it had been.

All the large firms reacted by moving away from their agricultural origins. For example, Ruston's in Lincoln found a profitable niche in earth-moving and quarrying equipment. Clayton & Shuttleworth's answer was the steam wagon. Perhaps it was not such a dreadful choice as it seems in retrospect: self-propelled road vehicles were indeed to increase massively in numbers, and at the time steam power was more cost-effective than the petrol engine. Shuttleworth believed that scale of production was essential. He also took the view that a capable and efficient engineering firm could turn its hand to other products when the market changed. He was partly correct in this: the firm was indeed able to use its skills and plant to produce aeroplanes on a massive scale in the First World War, as Charles Parker's chapter indicates; but when recession hit after the war it found that no one wanted to outsource production any longer.

To provide this new capacity, the massive Titanic Works was built, east of the existing Stamp End site. It was funded by selling the Austria-Hungary operation to its main competitor, Hoffherr & Schrantz, in 1911. That deal was in part a merger, the new firm there being known as Hoffherr-Schrantz-Clayton-Shuttleworth. Since the UK would be at war with Austria-Hungary three years later, the timing was rather fortuitous.

That war saw all the agricultural-engineering firms engaged heavily in defence production, with the corollary that they were unable to supply their normal customers. Those customers, in regions like South America, were able to turn to US suppliers. Usually they found them a satisfactory alternative. Thus, at the end of the war, the firms found that their traditional markets had largely disappeared: Europe was in a shattered condition and could rarely afford new purchases; in the UK, farmers had acquired tractors which they could use as a power source instead of steam; and other markets had been lost to the US. At first that did not matter: there was more than enough pent-up demand from non-agricultural users to keep works busy. In 1921 a recession followed. There were still orders for steam-wagons, but in nothing like the numbers that had been anticipated. The firm tried desperately to find new lines: battery-powered lorries were one product it tried, but the limited storage capacity of lead-acid batteries made these of use only for restricted applications. By 1929, a combine-harvester was produced: essentially a reaper with a small threshing machine incorporated. Like most US models at this date, it was not self-propelled and needed to be towed by a tractor. The trouble was that in a damp European climate the grain then needed to be put through a grain-dryer, something few farmers could afford to install. It was not the salvation some may have hoped for, and the firm went into receivership in 1929.

When the receivers came to make a distribution to creditors, they quite properly mentioned that the firm's assets included some debts owed by the (Imperial) Russian government which the Soviet Union had repudiated: if these were ever repaid, there would be scope for a further distribution. This has

Threshing in progress: note the number of men required. (*Ken Redmore collection*).

lodged in popular memory in the form 'Clayton & Shuttleworth failed because Russia would not pay its debts'. Such a narrative was undoubtedly comforting at a traumatic time, but it is simply untrue. Clayton & Shuttleworth failed because it was no longer a viable business. Of all the large industrial-engineering firms, Clayton & Shuttleworth was the only one to fail between the two wars. From the foregoing, it will be clear that the underlying cause was a bad strategic choice made in the Edwardian period, compounded by a neglect of innovation that went back to the 1860s.

The historian has to be wary of making judgements with the benefit of hindsight and of judging men or institutions by the standard of a different era. In this case it is possible to compare Clayton & Shuttleworth at Lincoln against their Vienna operation and to do so using two sources from before 1914. The first source is the booklet produced in 1907 to celebrate the golden jubilee of the Vienna branch, parts of which are accessible on the successor company's website. It is striking that the booklet is dominated by the internal-combustion engine and its applications; this was four years before Stamp End decided to focus on the steam wagon. Secondly, one finds that land adjacent to the branch's new works at Floridsdorf was used for a *trials ground*. We know from other sources that it was the practice at Vienna to dismantle specimens of their products that had seen many years' use to measure the amount of wear on moving parts. This sort of scientific measurement of a product's performance is not something one finds mentioned in any of the Lincoln sources. The second source comes from reminiscences written by the George Blakey, who was mentioned earlier. They were written in Austria during the First World War when he would have had no contact with Lincoln since 1914. He recalls how in the 1840s his father had been offered a partnership in the firm but declined (clearly afraid that the firm might fail, leading to his own financial ruin). The son regrets that decision 'for if their success had not spoiled me I should, if allowed, have put life into the business at a time it much needed it, as I did into [the] Vienna Branch when I got into power there.' That caveat, 'if... success had not spoiled me', is an interesting one: the founding partners *were* spoiled by success, in that they became too interested in things other than their business.

Duckering's Iron Foundry, 1845-1962

Mark Duckering

In 1845, Lincolnshire-born Richard Duckering, a 31-year-old moulder, and Edward Burton, a machine maker, went into business together, forming the partnership of Burton and Duckering – Iron and Brass Founders. Located close to their homes, at number 53½ Waterside South, they became one of the earliest iron founders in the city of Lincoln.

The three foundries of Ruston, Proctor and Company, of Burton and Duckering, and of Clayton and Shuttleworth were 'reached in turn along the riverside', according to one contemporary record. Examination of the nineteenth-century Padley plans of Lincoln suggest that the site of the Burton and Duckering works was in line with the later Montague Street footbridge that spanned the River Witham near Stamp End.

At the outset, Burton and Duckering seemed to be doing well, working alongside their employees, but they suffered a setback with the outbreak of a late-night fire, as reported in the *Stamford Mercury* on 3 September 1847:

> FIRE! Just before 11 o'clock on Monday night, 30th August, the foundry of Messrs Burton and Duckering burst all at once in a terrific blaze which enveloped the whole building. The County and City engines were speedily upon the spot, but the fire raged, all attempts to go inside the building to save the valuable models from destruction …. were utterly futile… and to hazard human life within its reach would have been madly courting disaster. The blaze being subdued after half an hour … The building was composed nearly entirely of wood and never ought to have been used for so dangerous a business as smelting and casting iron. The constant heat had dried out the wood and the roof crevices had filled with soot … this soot seemed at length to take fire like gunpowder and erupted in a magnificent coruscation and the fire in the interior having then obtained an upward vent raged like a furnace.

Fortunately, there were no casualties, as the workmen had left only 30 minutes before, but it had caused about £500 of uninsured damage to buildings and contents.

Very little was left after the fire but, as soon as tarpaulins and a kind of roof was erected, work began again, fulfilling orders for ovens, boilers, plough shares and machine castings. By 1855, the partnership had ended, with Richard Duckering continuing as sole employer. In 1856, Richard's

BURTON AND DUCKERING,
IRON AND BRASS FOUNDERS,
WATERSIDE SOUTH, LINCOLN.
Manufacturers of Ovens, Boilers and all kinds of Plough, Drill and Thrashing Machine Castings,
CONSTANTLY KEPT ON HAND.

Early advertisement in Leary's *Lincoln Guide and Advertiser,* 1848. (*Mark Duckering Collection*).

only son, Charles, aged 15, joined his father and around 25 employees. By 1857, the business had outgrown number 53½ Waterside South and so the larger Witham Steam Packet Company's former site was purchased on the north side of the river, including a coal-yard, offices, outbuildings and cottages, together with 429 square yards of land giving room for future expansion.

The move into the new foundry was made by 1859. The old buildings and cottages proved ideal as storage for the numerous patterns kept. Later, another 1000 square yards of land with four tenements, which the company had previously rented, was bought at auction in 1869 for £265.

In 1870, Richard died, aged 56 years, and 29-year-old Charles inherited, giving the business his name soon after. Within a decade he had erected a new warehouse (in 1874) and foundry on Rosemary Lane (in 1879), possibly fulfilling his late father's building application plan of 1869. Later applications were lodged for new offices on Waterside North (built in 1896), an extension to the packing shop on Croft Street (constructed in 1906) and a brand-new showroom on the corner of Rosemary Lane and Monks Road (erected in 1907).

Charles discovered the power of marketing and used it extensively in local papers, annuals, guides and directories, the majority with attractive illustrations of their manufactured implements. He gained further exposure by attending many of the county's agricultural shows and fairs, and the business had a twice-weekly presence at Lincoln's Cornhill and cattle market, these being a staple in the company's marketing agenda. As the *Lincolnshire Chronicle* noted on 21 July 1893: 'Duckering's was an extensive exhibitor whose machinery always drew a crowd.'

The same newspaper article drew attention to the types of items produced by Duckering's, ranging from saw benches, 'powered by hand, steam, horse or other motive power' to hay trussers, portable boilers and its award-winning 'Lincoln improved' grinding mills, 'some of which could be easily turned by a child'. The adaptability of these products made them increasingly in demand, both at home and abroad, and they were especially valuable where motive power was lacking.

Advertisement from *Lincolnshire Chronicle*, 21 April, 1896. (*Mark Duckering Collection*).

In December 1883, during a nationwide 'great storm', the top 8 to 10 feet of the company's distinctive 70-foot high chimney blew down and fell on to two cottages on neighbouring Commodore Close, injuring a family of four. The chimney had stood since the foundry was built in 1857. According to a report in the *Lincolnshire Chronicle* of 7 August 1885, the business was employing 'over 80 hands' at its iron and brass foundry at Waterside Works and was operating 'in the able hands of Charles Duckering'.

From the late 1880s into the early decades of the twentieth century, new and, for the time, fully-equipped homes sprang up to the east and west of Lincoln city centre, with Duckering's providing many items for the developers. Every kind of ironwork used by builders from the damp course to the roof was supplied by the company, including: pipework, guttering, ornate gates and fencing sets (in three designs), as well as fire grates, laundry stoves and its very popular cooking ranges. By 1920, a total of 30,000 cooking ranges had been sold by the company. Many of these Duckering-produced items still exist in properties in the Monks Road and Carholme Road areas, despite the removal of metal to aid the war effort in the 1940s.

In 1912, Charles retired after 50 years in the business, dying in 1916, and his son, Richard, took over the company and its debts. During the First World War, the company supplied parts for the newly-invented tank, which helped stave off bankruptcy. Business flourished and several hundred staff members were employed.

However, once the war was over, the industrial slump hit hard. Charles's grandson Dick Duckering, writing in 1983, noted that 'because of Richard's generosity at Christmas and many poor investments, including acquiring many small houses that soon generated into slums, he ran up a large overdraft'. This led Richard to sell the shop in September 1922 and, at around the same time, he turned the foundry business into a limited company. Four years later, Richard Duckering Ltd collapsed. The company's debts were finally settled with the sale of the family home. Richard Duckering then left Lincoln for good.

The business was taken over by the former works manager, Walter H. Freeman, who moved to the company in 1919. In April 1933 in the *Lincolnshire Chronicle*, he was described as 'a worthy successor to his predecessor'. He remained as chairman and managing director until his death in 1939, aged 62. Walter Freeman left the company on a sound footing and it continued to prosper during the war years following his death. The company's profits were used to fund improvements to the factory with the conversion of an old air-raid shelter into a washroom in 1947 and a new pattern shop built in 1948.

Duckering's shop and show rooms continued to operate throughout the war, regularly advertising in the local press as retailers of fireplaces, sanitary fittings and general hardware. In the immediate post-war years, Duckering's sought to cater to the needs of the city's more aspirational home owners. In the late 1940s, the company's advertisements encouraged customers to 'modernize your bathroom' so as to avoid 'embarrassment when you have guests'. It offered an 'extensive range of modern fireplaces' at its large showrooms at 25-33 Monks Road, and it proudly noted that it had supplied sanitary and bathroom equipment to the newly-opened Constance Stewart Hall at Lincoln Training College in October 1950, despite the 'difficult days of supply' that it mentioned in a Christmas advertisement later that year.

Percy G.M. Freeman, the son of Walter, was a member of the company's board at the time of his father's death. He continued his association with the company and, when he died in 1952, aged 47, he was running the operation. His widow, Gwendolen, took on the business, employing a manager in early 1954. After 12 months or so a new system for producing castings was introduced using gas to freeze the moulding sand. According to a former employee, Alex Wilcockson, speaking in 2005, this new process was one 'to which the management was 100% committed'. It required the 'irreversible modification of everything and every pattern box'. Two extensions were made to the moulding shop in 1954 and 1955 for this purpose. At the time, Duckering's largest client was the electrical engineering company Lancashire Dynamo and Crypto Company, based in Trafford Park, Manchester. Sadly, as Alex Wilcockson observed: 'this system failed miserably resulting in a poor final product and despite many attempts the required improvements couldn't be made – certainly not to Mr Freeman's standard. Subsequently the orders from Manchester dried up.'

The costs incurred in this venture and the loss of orders eventually led to the demise of the firm. In June 1962 it was announced, after 117 years, that Richard Duckering Ltd was going into voluntary liquidation. The Lincoln Y.M.C.A. and a Siemens' car park now occupy the site. Evidence of Duckering's manufacturing output, though, can still be seen across the city, as Arthur Ward's chapter on street furniture indicates.

Duckering's 'Waterside Works', depicted in an 1882 advertisement. (*Mark Duckering Collection*).

William Foster & Company

Andrew Walker

William Foster, born in Potter Hanworth in 1816, began business in partnership with John Hartley on Brayford Wharf East in 1845. The company was dissolved in 1848 and Foster alone acquired a flour-milling site at 42 Waterside North, east of City Iron and Wire Works. The land housed a substantial five-floor steam mill, a large five-bedroomed house, granaries, stables and pigsties. By 1852, as a newspaper report of a Christmas dinner at the *Durham Ox* provided by Foster for his workforce indicates, at least 80 people were employed by him. Alongside flour-milling activities, Foster started the manufacture of corn mills and thrashing machines. With the success of the engineering side of the business, flour milling ceased in 1856. The premises were swiftly expanded to encompass 42-45 Waterside North, with a foundry and additional workshops built. By 1900, the site occupied 4300 square yards, extending from Waterside North to St Rumbold Street.

Foster's first portable steam engine was built in 1858. The company developed a significant reputation for the production of these and also thrashing machines, winning a number of prizes in competitions. As the *Lincolnshire Chronicle* reported on 12 August 1859, for instance, a Foster's thrashing machine shared the first prize of £50 at the Highland Society's show, held in Edinburgh, with a competing machine entered by Robey's, another Lincoln-based company.

During the 1860s, Foster's regularly advertised its services in the local press as engineers, boilermakers and iron founders. Its product range included portable and fixed steam engines, thrashing machines, corn mills and sawing machinery. The business also sold a number of portable engines varying in size, and made chiefly by Clayton, Shuttleworth & Company. These products of a rival Lincoln company were described as being in 'thorough repair and are confidently recommended to anyone requiring a good cheap engine.' Foster's sales, though, reached well beyond the circulation district of the regional press. In 1869, branch works were opened in Budapest and Galtaz (in Romania). In 1871, Foster was recorded in the census as employing 68 men and 41 boys.

William Foster himself rose to some public prominence in the city. He served as a member of the Corporation as a representative of the Conservative Party. His admiration for the military leader, and later Tory Prime Minister, the Duke of Wellington, led to him naming his works in honour of the man, who died in 1852. In 1863-64, William Foster served as the city's mayor, following in the footsteps of his grandfather, and, for thirty years until his death he was an active board member of Lincoln's Lunatic Hospital at the Lawn. He was also the city's Chief Magistrate in 1863 and 1864, as mayor, though he was unable to serve as magistrate otherwise owing to his being a 'maltster on an extensive scale', as described in a council meeting in May 1863 at a time when the Liberal Lord Chancellor, Lord Westbury, who made these appointments, was known to have 'a strong objection to placing maltsters or brewers' in such posts. Foster's malting interests were actually based in Barton on Humber. In White's 1856 Lincolnshire Directory, he was listed as one of five maltsters in the town, and in the 1871 census he was described as being head of a firm of maltsters employing about 50 workers.

Foster died from typhoid in his home at Lindum Villas on Lindum Terrace, in 1876 at the age of 60. His death prompted much comment, not just eulogies about his accomplishments but also significant criticisms made of the city's authorities for their reluctance to address Lincoln's dire sanitation issues. As *The Lancet* declared in October 1876, the recent death of William Foster 'cannot but convey a reproach to the Town Council among whom he had for years laboured strenuously to supply the town with improved sanitary provision but was overruled in his laudable efforts by an obstructive majority.'

Foster's business continued to thrive despite his death and, in 1877, it became a limited company, William Foster & Company. In 1883, with the company outgrowing its site, and with no immediate access to the railway, it bought five acres of land from the Ellison family to the west of the city, on the 'Derby Grounds', next to the main railway line to Nottingham. A long complex of workshops for the manufacture of thrashing machines and other implements was erected, together with a saw mill and wood-drying sheds. By 1885, they were in full operation, with the company now employing some 200 workers. A foundry and blacksmith's shop were also constructed on the site. The new buildings were erected by the Lincoln building firm of Otter and Broughton and had been designed by city-based architects Goddard and Son. This new location was principally home to the wood-working aspects of the business, with the occupation of the original site continuing as well until 1900. In addition to thrashing machines, the product range of the company comprised a wide range of agricultural-related equipment including chaff cutters, hay stackers, maize shellers, corn grinders as well as fixed engines, boilers and saw benches. In 1889, the company's first steam traction engine was built.

The opportunity was taken to consolidate the company's operations on a single site in 1898. An additional six acres of land was purchased adjoining the Derby Grounds site. By May 1900, the company's operations at Waterside North were fully relocated to the newly-built facilities, now known as the Wellington Foundry, occupying an area over five times as large as the previous site. The new purpose-built accommodation allowed full use to be made of the railways, with all of the raw materials being transported by rail and the vast majority of finished products were then conveyed to customers by train. A detailed 2000-word description of the new facilities, now employing 400 workers, was included in the *Lincolnshire Chronicle* on 6 July 1900. Much emphasis was placed within the report on the modern nature of the plant, and particularly the extensive use of electrical power throughout the complex, ranging from lighting to the driving of individual machines. It was noted that only the saw mill continued to be powered by steam. The electrical power was generated on site, using two dynamos each of 150 brake horse power.

The new general offices were approached from Firth Road. Mess rooms were provided for the workers and, perhaps inspired by the cleaner air now possible in the works as a result of the use of electric power, smokers and non-smokers were offered separate mess accommodation. The works was divided into four separate divisions – the well-established wood side and three other newly-built sections, the iron side, smiths' department and foundry department.

It was noted by the reporter that, on the wood side of the works, in production were thrashing machines, elevators, maize shellers, chaff cutters, and traction wagons to be sold in many parts of world. The timber used accordingly needed to be well seasoned to withstand varied climatic conditions. The journalist saw many large stacks of timber, which had been seasoning from eight to nine years. He noted: 'We were shown one piece of evidence of the stability and durability of the manufactures in the form of a letter just received, in which a client asked for a new crank shaft for a thrashing machine manufactured by Messrs. Foster & Co., and supplied to the writer's father no fewer than forty years ago!' The reporter concluded by noting that a number of the company's products were exported to Germany. He commented: 'This fact itself is evidence of the excellence of the manufactures, for is not Germany amongst the greatest of our industrial rivals?'

The former site of Foster's works on Waterside North was sold at auction in May 1900 for £4100 to Rainforth & Company. The new owners quickly sought to redevelop it to their needs by issuing a tender in September 1900 for the demolition of the flour mill and advertised some of the superfluous land for sale, referring to the 'old' Wellington Foundry. Rainforth's is examined in a separate chapter by Adam Cartwright.

At its newly-expanded works the product range of Foster's increased, especially under its new general manager, William Tritton, who was appointed in 1906 and then promoted to Managing Director in 1911, a post he held until 1939, when he became Chairman of the company. At the 1907 Royal Show, held on the West Common in Lincoln, William Foster & Company's trade stand comprised a selection of road hauling engines, including a number of lighter-weight road locomotives designed to comply with new legislation, weighing in at under 14 tons. The firm's Wellington compound steam tractor received much attention. In the agricultural section of the company's exhibition space were displayed several traction engines, chaff cutters and heavy and light weight traction wagons. There was also room for a vertical high-speed engine, supplied largely for ship lighting plants.

Whippet tanks under construction at the Wellington Works, 1917. *(Courtesy of the John Wilson Collection, Saxilby History Group).*

As the company switched to a military footing following the outbreak of the Great War, many of the company's haulage-related products had a direct applicability to the war effort, particularly in the transportation of heavy artillery. At the time of the tank's development from 1915, for which William Foster & Company is renowned, the company was the only one manufacturing commercially caterpillar-tracked vehicles.

In early 1915 the War Office began experimenting with various 'trench-crossing' vehicles, including a machine designed by William Tritton. The Government set up a Landships Committee in February 1915, chaired by Winston Churchill as First Lord of the Admiralty. Although the first trench crossers failed to work effectively, William Tritton was asked to design a machine, using caterpillar tracks on an armoured car. A new machine, nicknamed 'Little Willie' was produced by the end of 1915. Further refinements were made, partly in an attempt to improve the machine's mobility and the first of the 'Big Willie' machines was made, which, perhaps rather confusingly, then became known as 'Mother'. This was the first of the 'female' tanks, which carried several machine guns, whereas the 'male' variant was equipped with a mix of machine guns and cannons.

The workers involved in the production of these machines, including many women, were told, for security reasons, that they were constructing 'water tanks for Mesopotamia,'. The Landships Committee was soon renamed, by December 1915, the Tank Supply Committee.

Tanks were in full production in Lincoln by 1916, and their design was speedily amended with their use in the war. The machines were tested near to Foster's factory on what is now Tritton Road. Other First World War types of tank designed in Lincoln, with some built in the city, included the Mark IV; the Whippet, which was lighter and faster, achieving speeds of 9 miles per hour; and the last tank to be designed at Foster's in Lincoln was the Horne, which possessed an all-round field of fire.

Along with Lieutenant Walter Gordon Wilson, who was responsible for the development of the tank's engine, William Tritton received £15,000 from the Royal Commission on Awards to Inventors following the war for his important part in the invention of the tank. Tritton had already been knighted in 1917 for his part in the development and production project management of this important military development. Whilst it is important to highlight the essential contribution of William Foster & Company in the design and development of the tank, it should be noted that the majority of First World War tanks were built elsewhere in Britain, by other companies, such as the Birmingham-based Metropolitan Amalgamated Railway Carriage and Wagon Company Ltd (later to become Metro-Cammell), which alone produced 1100 examples. During the First World War, Britain manufactured 2636 tanks in total, compared to France's 3870.

As with many other engineering companies in Lincoln and indeed across Britain, Foster's found the inter-war years challenging times in which to operate. Tank production ceased with the end of the war. The international market, in which Foster's had traded extensively, shrank significantly. The company was relatively slow to respond to changing technological developments. Indeed, the company was still producing traction engines until 1942. The company acquired Gwynne's Engineering Company in 1927, which was in liquidation. Gwynne's had been a company at which Sir William Tritton had served his apprenticeship.

Women munition workers in front of a 'male' Mark IV tank, c. 1917. Timber in the yard of Ruston, Proctor & Company's Sheaf Wood Works is clearly visible in the background. The tank is probably 'Lurcher', number 2397, which was used for a similar photograph of male workers, where its serial number was displayed. (*Courtesy of the John Wilson Collection, Saxilby History Group*).

A new company Gwynne's Pumps was formed, owned by William Foster & Company and made Lincoln its base, with William Tritton as its chairman. Its principal product lines were gravel dredgers, and hydraulic drainage pumps, catering for the needs of water management in mines, sewers and fenland settings.

In 1961, W.H. Allen and Sons and Company acquired both William Foster & Company and Gwynne's Pumps. The Wellington Foundry closed in 1968, but was then occupied by Ruston Bucyrus and Ruston Gas Turbines until demolition took place in 1983-84. The site is now part of a retail park. A plaque on the Morrison's supermarket site commemorates the work that took place near there by William Foster & Company, and especially William Tritton, specifically the design, production and testing of the prototype tank in 1915; the name of Tritton Road ensures the company's managing director is remembered and, in 2015, the year of its centenary, a tank memorial was unveiled at the roundabout at the north end of Tritton Road, as detailed in the chapter by Heather Hughes and Tom Kitchen.

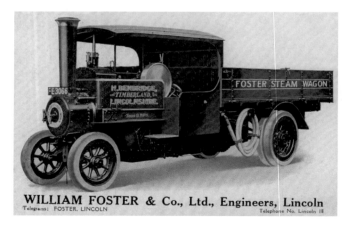

Foster's steam wagon, 1920 in the livery of Harry Pembridge, farmer of Timberland. (*Courtesy of the John Wilson Collection, Saxilby History Group*).

John Cooke & Sons

Hugh Cooke

During the second half of the nineteenth century, John Cooke's Lindum Plough Works became Lincoln's largest manufacturer of agricultural carts and wagons, and the largest plough maker in Lincolnshire, with business throughout the country and overseas. John Cooke was born at Eagle in 1821, apprenticed locally and, by 1841, was working as a wheelwright and plough maker in Eagle. He set up his own plough-making business in 1852 and, in 1854, at the Royal Agricultural Society implement trials in Lincoln, the performance of Mr. Cooke's general purpose plough was described as excellent.

By February 1858, John Cooke had moved his business from Eagle to premises near to the newly-opened Lincoln Cattle Market, on Monks Lane, which was renamed Monks Road in October 1859. In 1861, John Cooke was trading as an implement maker, specialising in 'Prize Ploughs', producing some 2000 ploughs annually, and living at 21 Monks Road with his young family, very near his business premises. The increasing sales of ploughs led to an enlargement of the premises, which was advertised in February 1866.

John Cooke's Plough Works had moved into new, larger premises by 1871. The factory was well placed to attract the attention of farmers attending the Cattle Market on Monks Road, lying between Rosemary Lane and Montague Street, and extending down to Croft Street. A plough was mounted on the Monks Road boundary wall to advertise the factory's principal output. Now named the Lindum Plough Works, the large red brick-built works were equipped to meet the demand for consignments of ploughs with interchangeable spares for shipping to the colonies and to South America. The site was later developed even further. These improvements included the construction of a paint shop, in 1873, and the erection of an additional large shed, constructed in 1886. Cooke's ploughs were renowned for the attention paid to high-quality materials and consistent processing. The chill-casting of the shares was an essential technology in the new factory. Whilst ploughs were the principal product, John Cooke produced many other farm implements and a range of carts, and 'hermaphrodite' wagons. Lincolnshire 'moffreys' were rugged two-wheeled carts, for general work, which

Letterhead of John Cooke's Lindum Plough Works, 1883, illustrating the company's products and its premises. The yard, with ploughs on display, adjoins the south side of Monks Road. The correspondence is addressed to Lincoln's newly-appointed City Surveyor, R.A. McBrair. (*Ken Redmore Collection*).

Cooke's Colonial double-furrow plough. The company first produced double-furrow ploughs in 1870. (*Ken Redmore Collection*).

could be converted to four-wheeled wagons for carrying hay or cereals.

The Plough Works' wage-book for 1864 to 1866 shows employee numbers rising from 15 to 24, most working a full six-day week. About one-third of the workforce were skilled men earning over £1 per week, about one-third were semi-skilled, earning between 10 shillings and £1, and the labourers each received under 10 shillings a week. There was a considerable demand for skilled workmen at this time of rapid industrial growth in Lincoln, and John Cooke was paying wages which appear to have been competitive.

John Cooke's patented construction of the single-beam plough, using angle-iron and wood, was introduced during the 1860s. The report in *The Implement and Machinery Review* of August 1878 stated that this was a 'combination that not only lightens and cheapens the implement, but also gives to it an amount of strength otherwise unobtainable in many different forms.' The author of this report complimented Mr Cooke on the superior appearance of his implements and received the reply – 'Well, they ought to look nice, for I personally examine everything before it leaves the works.'

Ploughing matches provided an excellent opportunity to compare the performances of all of the major plough makers' products. John Cooke's ploughs achieved a high reputation and were competing with five considerable companies. Hornsby of Grantham was the company's only local rival; the others were all located in adjoining counties. *The Implement and Machinery Review* in August 1878 reported that Cooke's was showing 20 ploughs at the Royal Agricultural Society's exhibition at Bristol and, in August 1879, as many as 34 'splendid samples' were displayed at the Royal Agricultural Society's show in Kilburn, north London. John Cooke's products received many medals and awards at the major agricultural shows over the years.

Extract from John Cooke's Illustrated Catalogue of 1876:

> *John Cooke has much pleasure in submitting this Catalogue to the notice of Agriculturists and the public generally, and embraces the opportunity to inform them that he has made the manufacture of **Ploughs** his **speciality** and **study** for upwards of **thirty years**, during which time he has gained such an amount of practical experience in this department as probably few men have, and which, he ventures to think, entitles him to the fullest confidence of his patrons.*

*He also begs to announce that his Works are still under his own **personal supervision** and **direction**, and that his manufactures may therefore be thoroughly relied upon as regards **quality** and **efficiency**, and to properly perform the work for which they were intended; great **care** being taken as to the **excellence** of the **workmanship** and the **suitability** and **durability** of the **materials** employed.*

*J.C. would draw the special attention of **merchants** and **shippers**, &c., to the fact that he possesses unusual facilities for manufacturing large **quantities** of **Ploughs** of any description on the **shortest notice**, having a large plant and staff almost solely engaged in making Ploughs.*

When John Cooke died suddenly in 1887, aged 66, the management of the firm was taken over by his son, Frank, who was 26 years old. There is no record of his two brothers having any further involvement with the company.

There were about 70 employees at the time Frank Cooke inherited the firm. When he died in 1922 there were some 100 workers employed by the company. The fact that Frank Cooke's funeral was attended by a large number of employees, many of whom had worked for the business for over 30 years, was remarked on in his obituary as indicating the excellent industrial relations that prevailed at the company.

After Frank Cooke's death the company was managed by his elder son Sidney Cooke, with Frank's younger son, Horace, looking after the sales side. John Cooke & Sons was put into receivership in March 1938 with between 60 and 70 staff. At the closing auction Edlington's of Gainsborough bought the stock and patterns. Edlington's continued to manufacture some of Cooke's designs and to provide spares for Cooke's products into the 1950s.

A farm dray manufactured by John Cooke & Sons, 1909. (*Ken Redmore Collection*).

ROBEY & COMPANY

Adam Cartwright

Early in 1854, Nottingham-born Robert Robey entered into partnership with William Watkinson, a foreman from Clayton & Shuttleworth's works. They acquired a former tobacco factory in St Rumbold's Lane, just off Broadgate, and by July that year were able to enter into trials at the Royal Agricultural Show their 'plain, sound-looking' 8 horse-power steam engine 'very creditable to beginners in the trade'. George Scott, previously a foreman at the Sharpe Stewart locomotive works in Manchester, joined the partnership that December, and although Watkinson left a month later, in little over a year Robey and Scott had made so much progress that they were able to export a 10 horse-power, one-cylinder steam engine to the Crimea; from drawing board to production had taken just over one month.

By January 1857, Robert Robey was in partnership with Thomas Gamble, Scott too having gone his own way. They had outgrown the tobacco factory, and moved to new premises off Canwick Road, with a grand-sounding name – the Perseverance Iron Works – which remained the firm's base for 131 years. The firm added thrashing machines, boilers and pumps to its product range, and in 1860 built its first traction engine, tested that June by hauling a wagon containing 20 men up Canwick Hill. Robey's became so successful that the workforce grew from 114 men and boys, recorded in the 1861 census, to 503 listed ten years later.

Robert Robey quickly became a rich man, but not without personal sadness. His first wife Emma died in 1863, leaving him a widower with 7 children. He became, with other local industrialists, the target of election rioters in the city, who damaged his home at 367 High Street, in July 1865, and probably encouraged him to build a new and much larger home, Portland House, away from the city centre on South Park. In 1869 he was cited as a co-respondent in an embarrassing divorce case. He became seriously ill in 1873 and moved from Lincoln back to Nottingham, where he died aged only 50 in March 1876. He is buried in Canwick cemetery, his grave referring to his death after 'three years of suffering'.

Robert Robey left the business in excellent hands; a revised partnership continued the trade, with financial support from local businessmen. Key partners in Robey's from this point included Frederick Clench, the works manager, Thomas Bell, the long-serving secretary, and John Richardson, who was a highly-skilled engineer and inventor.

Robey & Company's erecting shop at the Globe Works, 1892. (*Source: Grace's Guide*).

Robey & Company's compound horizontal engines installed at Newcastle-on-Tyne Electric Supply Company, 1899. (*Source: Grace's Guide*).

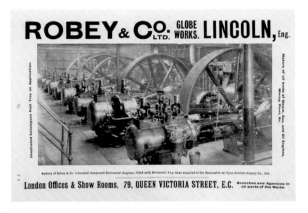

Richardson was the guiding hand behind many of Robey's new ventures. These included its patented 'undertype' engine of 1873 (a fixed engine and boiler combination, the cylinders bolted under the boiler) and even a small number of industrial railway locomotives (from the 1870s) for its burgeoning export market. Robey's international success, with sales agencies abroad in Budapest, Wroclaw and Johannesburg, was reflected in the new Globe Works name which was applied to its Canwick Road site from 1881 (displacing the original Perseverance branding). The works gradually expanded eastward, eventually occupying over 12 acres, so that by 1884 about 900 men were employed there, consolidating Robey's status as Lincoln's third largest employer after Ruston's and Clayton's. The firm was a relatively benevolent employer, providing a new mess room and coffee house in 1884, the latter a nod to the teetotal enthusiasms of several Robey partners. In 1893 the company claimed to have supplied over 14,000 engines and boilers alone to customers worldwide.

As the old century drew to an end, like many others at the time, Robey's formed a private limited company, established in 1893 with initial issued share capital of £272,710 and £125,000 offered in debenture loan stock. By this time the company had a London office at 79 Queen Victoria Street, and its own branches abroad as mentioned above, as well as many other international agencies. As the business approached maturity, some of the older figures left the scene. Fredrick Clench departed when the new company was formed, and John Richardson resigned a few weeks after the death of Thomas

An optimistic advertisement from 1943 outlining Robey & Company's proposed post-war product ranges. (*Source: Grace's Guide*).

The surviving Robey & Company's Globe Works insignia, Canwick Road. (*Andrew Walker*).

Bell in 1905, ostensibly on the grounds that he felt new board members were needed. Richardson had long been a controversial figure: his engineering brilliance had to be balanced against his unbending commitment to teetotalism, Methodism and eventually politics: some trenchant remarks he made at a public meeting about what he saw as the plight of the Boers had caused great alarm to the company, South Africa being a key market.

Following the outbreak of the First World War, Robey's followed Ruston's into production of military aircraft, and eventually the company supplied some 300 warplanes, including a number of sea planes. Nearly all of its production was subcontracted from more established manufacturers, but Robey's was the only Lincoln firm to produce its own designs of aircraft, led by J. A. Peters, the company's chief designer. The Robey-Peters RRF25 'Fighting Machine', an impressively-armed, three-seater aircraft, first flew in September 1916 but only two prototypes were produced and both were destroyed during flight testing at Bracebridge Heath. The Robey seaplane seems not to have gone beyond the design stage, and unfortunately no Robey-built aircraft are known to survive. More details regarding Robey's involvement in aircraft manufacture can be found in Charles Parker's chapter.

Robey's resumed peacetime production, turning the former aircraft works over to the manufacture of steam wagons, which it first produced in 1906. The company launched a more successful overtype design in 1919, which became a highly popular product both at home and abroad, its manufacture lasting until 1934 – in fact, two preserved examples in Sri Lanka were still in occasional use as late as the 1980s. Colliery winding engines were another important Robey product of the period, powerful stationary steam engines with complicated valve gear which powered mining hoists. A winder built by Robey's for Linby Colliery in

Nottinghamshire in 1922 and used for 60 years can now be seen at Papplewick Pumping Station museum, and other Robey winders are believed still to be in use in other countries.

Robey's was just one of many businesses to suffer from the economic downturn of the inter-war years; as early as 1929 the Midland Bank expressed concern about the company's overdraft and profitability. The sale of the Johannesburg branch and premises, a moratorium on debenture interest and an increase in Robey's overdraft to £52,000, only sadly, delayed the eventual appointment of a receiver in May 1933. But Robey's bounced back, having reached an accommodation with its creditors, and in 1935 the board regained control. The works were again turned over to military production in the 1940s, but no aircraft were manufactured this time: Robey's instead produced a wide range of machinery including naval steam engines, gun mountings and ammunition hoists. Post-war, Robey's concentrated on boilers and winders, but remained able to turn its expertise to specialised products as well – even parts for the Jodrell Bank telescope.

In 1985 Robey's was acquired by Babcock International, which was in turn bought by FKI Electricals of Loughborough, a much smaller business. FKI embarked on a restructuring

Detail of Robey & Company's Globe Works, Canwick Road. (*Andrew Walker*).

programme, which included selling off a number of manufacturing assets, leading to the closure of Robey's in February 1988. The Globe Works site is now occupied by the builders' merchants Buildbase (formerly Jackson's). Much of the Canwick Road frontage has been retained, with an original doorway with a globe carved into the stonework, although many of the works buildings have been demolished. Robey's also lives on in another way as the Robey Trust, a charity based at Tavistock in Devon, set up in 1983 following the donation by the town's council of a Robey Tandem Roller to a group of enthusiastic restorers. Damaged and corroded after 20 years in a playground, the roller was restored over a seven-year period. The charity is now devoted to the restoration and preservation of the company's products.

Detail of Robey & Company's Globe Works, Canwick Road. (*Andrew Walker*).

From Ruston, Burton & Proctor to Ruston, Proctor & Co. Ltd, 1857-1900

Lesley Clarke

This chapter traces the journey of the company bearing the name of 'Ruston' from its beginnings in a small shed on the swampy ground of Waterside South to the end of the nineteenth century, by which time it was a large and successful operation. As Chris Page notes in his earlier chapter, by 1840 James Toyne Proctor, a millwright, had partnered John Burton, a blacksmith, and, after John's death in 1842, his brother and fellow blacksmith, Theophilus Burton. Proctor and Burton (sometimes referred to as Burton and Proctor) became established as millwrights and engineers. The company's works at 52 Waterside South had access to the River Witham for transporting raw materials and finished products. The workshop was a shed in a tiny corner of the site which would become the Sheaf Iron Works. The land was leased from Lincoln Corporation and had to be raised in level as it was swampy and prone to flooding. There, they produced ploughs and harrows, and also assembled and maintained portable steam engines, but they did not make all the parts themselves. Both Proctor and Burton were highly-skilled craftsmen. However, they lacked the drive to expand their small business and looked for another partner to help them. This was to be Joseph Ruston, a 22-year-old living in Sheffield. Although Ruston was ultimately extremely successful, his enthusiasm, energy and perceived risk-taking were to prove too much for both Proctor and Burton.

Ruston entered into negotiations with Proctor and Burton in 1856. Although their business was small, Ruston recognised the quality of their products and agreed to enter into partnership with them. On 1 January 1857 the partnership of Proctor and Burton was dissolved, making way for the new firm of Ruston, Burton and Proctor, placing Ruston in the forefront of the company where he was to have complete control of the commercial side of the business. Ruston immediately started planning to expand the company, looking for more land to extend the works and ordering the building of two portable steam engines to go into stock: a revolutionary idea as equipment had always been made to order. His enthusiasm soon proved too much for the cautious Burton, and, after only four months, on 1 May 1857, the partnership of Ruston, Burton and Proctor was dissolved. On 18 July 1857 Burton sold his share in the company for £855 10s, a third of the estimated value of the business. The company was then re-named Ruston, Proctor & Company. Ruston continued adding more items to stock, a venture which proved successful.

Britain was entering a period of the long 'agricultural revolution', referred to by some as the steam age of farming, which would give many opportunities for those willing to pursue them. An increasing population required more food and agricultural workers were leaving the land to seek work in urban factories. Both factors created a need for more agricultural machines, and Joseph Ruston believed in their future, both in Britain and worldwide. Ruston's foresight would lead his company to become one of the major producers of agricultural machinery. For some time, the success of the business depended on the state of agricultural harvests at home and abroad; a bad harvest would produce few orders, whereas a good one, when its machines would be in demand, would be profitable.

The arrival of the railways in the mid-nineteenth century was also a major contributing factor in the development of engineering industries in Lincoln, adding to the waterways and roads already available and leading the city into a new era of industry. In Kelly's 1861 Directory the company is listed as 'engineers, millwrights & agricultural machine makers' and the premises described as 'Sheaf Iron Works, Waterside South'. By this time the number of employees had risen to 135 men and boys.

In 1863, Joseph Ruston and James Proctor bought land in the parish of St Peter at Gowts. Proctor transferred his interest in this to Ruston in 1865, the year in which he retired from the company. Although the company was successful he, like Burton, could not keep up with the energy and enthusiasm of the younger Ruston. For the sake of tradition and goodwill the name of the company remained as Ruston, Proctor & Co. – although added in brackets after this title was 'J. Ruston, Sole Proprietor'.

Ruston, Proctor & Co continued to expand, and, in 1865, established a dedicated woodworking site – the Sheaf Wood Works – in Anchor Street. The site was on an area of waste land to

the south of the city centre, in the parish of St Peter at Gowts, which as it expanded south and west became known as New Boultham. Joseph Ruston continued to buy parcels of land in this area on various dates until 1879. Other companies became established there and a new industrial area was created.

A portable 10 horse-power Ruston Proctor steam engine manufactured in 1884. It has been named 'Jack' and is displayed in the Museum of Lincolnshire Life. (*Richard Still*).

An advertisement for Ruston, Proctor & Company, displaying a range of products in action and the company's recent prizes at the 1900 Paris Exhibition, where it won gold awards relating to both mechanical and civil engineering. (*Courtesy of the John Wilson Collection, Saxilby History Group*).

From the 1870s, the company was also producing non-agricultural products – locomotives, traction engines, steamrollers, and the mighty Dunbar-Ruston Steam Navvy in 1875. These were the first mechanical excavators to be built in Lincoln and many were extensively used in the construction of the Manchester Ship Canal.

The freehold of the land on Waterside South was purchased from Lincoln Corporation in 1876. In addition, Joseph Ruston is recorded as buying various parcels of land between 1865 and 1884 in the parish of St Swithin, which included Waterside South. Immediately to the east were the Stamp End Iron Works of the larger firm of Clayton & Shuttleworth.

In 1885, the Institution of Mechanical Engineers reported on its members' visit to both the Sheaf Iron and Wood Works, noting that the company then employed 1400 hands and covered 13 acres, the two sites being half a mile apart. By 1886 the Sheaf Iron Works had spread further south, across the Sincil Dyke.

In 1889, when the company had 1600 employees, Ruston converted it into a public company – Ruston, Proctor & Co. Ltd. The direction of the company remained the same, with Ruston continuing as chairman. On 6 November 1889, Joseph Ruston transferred his ownership of the Sheaf Iron Works and the Sheaf Wood Works to Messrs Ruston, Proctor & Co. Ltd.

On 2 June 1893 the *Lincolnshire Chronicle* published a report on the fourth annual ordinary general meeting of the company, stating that it was held in the 'large new Mess-room at the Sheaf Iron Works, Lincoln'. Ruston wished the meeting to be held there to show off the new dining room, although he apologised for the noise from their neighbours, Messrs. Doughty, Son and Richardson. The exterior of this staff facility, plans for which were produced by the company in July 1892, alongside those for a Time Office, where wage payments were managed, can still be seen. Immediately east of Doughty's 1863 oil mill is a red-brick building with the words, just discernible, over a blocked doorway 'RUSTON N.. DINING HALL' (the second word is partially covered by an alarm). This, and similar buildings running east along Waterside South towards the remains of a Clayton & Shuttleworth building, are now part of Siemens' Ruston Works. Nothing remains of the Sheaf Wood Works (which later became known as the Anchor Street Works). The site has since been developed and is now mainly residential.

The death of Joseph Ruston took place late on the evening of Thursday 10 June 1897 at his home, Monks' Manor. By the time of his death the small millwrights' shop employing 25 hands that he had joined in 1857 had grown to become a large engineering establishment with 2550 employees, covering an area of 17 acres, which had brought worldwide fame to Lincolnshire engineering. In 1901, Ruston's elder son Colonel Joseph Seward Ruston became chairman of the company and the name of Ruston would remain with the firm until the late 1980s when Ruston Gas Turbines was acquired by European Gas Turbines. The later history of the company is covered in part in two subsequent chapters, by Abi Hunt and Derek Broughton.

Ruston Proctor & Company employees in one of the works' yards, c. 1900. The company had a workforce of 4303 in 1909, including 3950 workmen, and 60 head foremen who wore distinctive bowler (also known as billycock) hats. One of these head foremen can be seen in the front row. (*Courtesy of the John Wilson Collection, Saxilby History Group*).

Benjamin Taplin, Joseph Lee and the Patent Crank and Traction Engine Works

Nicholas Moore

In the mid-1850s great excitement was being created by the idea that self-propelled or traction engines could equal, on roads, the success that was being enjoyed by railways. In 1857 a 'traction engine and endless railway', invented by James Boydell, had drawn in three days a heavily-loaded wagon train over 85 miles of road from Thetford to Acton on the outskirts of London. Boydell's patent engines were manufactured by Burrell's of Thetford and by Tuxford's at Boston. Other makers of road locomotives and traction engines were William Bray of Deptford, London, and Thomas Aveling of Rochester in Kent. Aveling had fitted cranks and drive shafts with a chain-driven main wheel to a portable steam engine, made by Clayton and Shuttleworth of Lincoln.

These developments must have been closely watched by Joseph Lee. Having been born in Northampton, he described himself as an 'engineer' and in 1851 he was living in Cambridge. The 1861 census records some of his children as being born in Wolverhampton, a centre of the metalworking trades, so he presumably came directly from there, before moving to Lincoln in 1858 or early in 1859. In Lincoln, he entered into a partnership with Adam Borland, a Lincoln draper, to run the Norman Street foundry, on a site just off Sincil Street.

Lee had been developing a machine for producing engine cranks. These had previously been laboriously hand-forged, and the new machine promised a much easier means of production to a higher standard of precision. Lee received a patent in February 1859 for his machine for producing cranks. However, an acrimonious dispute developed between Lee and Borland and the partnership was dissolved in October of that year.

Lee now needed another business partner as he was developing the idea that his cranks could be used in the construction of a traction engine. He found a partner in Dr Benjamin Taplin, a young surgeon, born in Newark in 1831, who had a medical practice, with Dr Glazier, at 264 High Street. Lee also received support from others, including Joseph Ruston and Michael Penistan. Taplin took over the management of the enterprise.

At first, Lee and Taplin were making 8 horse-power

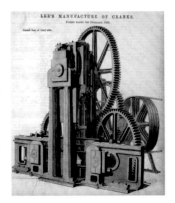

Lee's patent machine for the manufacture of cranks, as shown in *The Engineer*, **23 September 1859.** (*Source: Grace's Guide*).

The Taplin & Lee 16hp traction engine exhibited at the Great International Exhibition of 1862, as illustrated in the accompanying catalogue. (*Source: Grace's Guide*).

traction engines and portable engines, intended for steam ploughing and driving threshing machines. They may also have manufactured threshing machines. They acquired the premises of the Lincoln Beetroot Distillery in St Peter at Gowts parish, on the bank of the River Witham, which was approached from the *Blue Anchor* on the High Street. Today, it is near the site of the Royal Mail sorting office. New machinery was bought in to equip the works. By August 1860 the firm was advertising from the 'Patent Crank Works'.

Having equipped the foundry at St Peter at Gowts, Taplin and Company had started production of engines by May 1861, when it exhibited a 8 horse-power traction engine at the Bath and West of England Agricultural Society's show at Truro. This was followed by the company exhibiting at the Derbyshire Agricultural Society's first show at Derby in September 1861, when their traction engine was awarded a silver medal and first prize in its class. The traction engine that was exhibited at the Royal Agricultural Show at Leeds in July 1861 was described in *Bell's Weekly Messenger* on 22 July 1861. It noted that:

> It is fitted with a single cylinder, link motion, and the traction gear is so simple as only to require the driver of an ordinary portable engine to direct it. Also fitted with a tank, which is capable of holding 75 gallons of water, and the space for coals sufficient for five miles' journey.

The novelty of Taplin's traction engines was recorded in an account of the North Lincolnshire Agricultural Show, held at Brigg in August 1861, when 'Taplin and Co., Lincoln' exhibited both its traction-engine and patent cranks for locomotives. It was reported in *Bell's Weekly Messenger* on 5 August 1861 that:

> The engine amused the visitors by travelling round the field at intervals during the day, and on two occasions passed through Brigg with a thrashing machine attached to the wonderment of the uninitiated, but to the satisfaction of those who are pretty well versed in machinery.

Taplin and Lee were ambitious and, by autumn 1861, were producing a larger, 12 horse-power traction engine of a much more advanced design. It was described in *Bell's Weekly Messenger* on 25 November 1861 as:

> one of Taplin and Co.'s Double Cylinder Traction Engines of 12 Horse Power, fitted with their Patent Traction Gear, Steering, Raising, and Lowering Apparatus, to regulate the height of water on the Fire Box when travelling on irregular roads or fields. Is fitted with a Water Tank, and space for Coals sufficient for a long journey.

The engine was driven in the opposite direction with a driver standing with his back to the fireman. The wheels were made from iron and the power was provided by cogs engaging with the driving wheels. This vehicle was clearly intended for drawing heavy loads on roads.

While Taplin and Lee had spotted a market for these powerful vehicles, they were too late to make a commercial success from them. The public, and particularly the turnpike trusts, worried about the damage that would ensue to roads and bridges from these heavy vehicles passing over them. Bills had been presented to Parliament in 1859 and 1860 to regulate traction engines on public roads, but had not been passed. The Bill was brought forward again in 1861, and was being considered by the House of Lords, when, on 21 June, the *Evening Standard* reported a 'FEARFUL OMNIBUS ACCIDENT' on Hampstead Hill. This involved one of Bray's Traction Engines, which collided with a horse-drawn omnibus that subsequently overturned, killing two people and injuring many of the passengers. This led to the first Highways Act, passed on 1 August 1861. Amongst the stipulations in the Act were that these vehicles should be controlled by two men. It was followed by the Second Highways Act or 'Red Flag' Act of 1865, imposing speed limits of 2mph in London and 4mph in rural areas, with the requirement that the vehicle should be proceeded by a man carrying a red flag.

Taplin received great praise for his 8 horse-power traction engine at the Smithfield Show in London at the start of December 1861. This was reported in the *Morning Chronicle* on 11 December 1861 and the article was widely syndicated throughout the national press. The paper related that, amongst the 30 or so portable engines on display:

> there was one traction engine, much less in size and cost, but of great power, suitable for all general purposes the farmer now requires—such as ploughing, thrashing, drawing heavy weights behind it, up and down hill, and on uneven roads, without the aid of horses, that has been so great a drawback to the progress of steam cultivation. This noble traction engine was awarded the first prize and silver medal at the Derby Agricultural Meeting, to manufacturers, Messrs. Taplin and Co., of Lincoln.

It was also noted that:

> as we pass on towards the entrance [of the exhibition] we find drawings and plans of the new steam plough, invented and patented by Mr. Wm. Stevens, also manufactured by Messrs. Taplin Co. Lincoln. This steam plough is intended to work with the new traction engine that we have noticed above, and it appears is being made under practical experience regardless of expense, and with a determination to bring the implement required for steam ploughing and cultivation of the simple and effective, that they may safely be entrusted to the care and management of intelligent farm labourers.

Mr Stevens had already supplied a set of these steam ploughs to Prince Albert for cultivation on the royal farms at Windsor and it was predicted that these ploughs would take a prominent position in the 'Great Exhibition of Nations' to be held the following year.

Taplin, possibly greatly encouraged by the complimentary comments he was receiving in the press, launched a widespread advertising campaign, with woodcut illustrations of his engines, in many regional newspapers. According to the catalogue for the Great International Exhibition in 1862, the 12 horse-power traction engine was sold for £425 and Taplin also built a 16 horse-power version, which he offered for £590. He made the claim that traction engines up to 50 horse-power could be built to order.

However, at the Bath and West Show, also in May 1862, Taplin's traction engines were illustrated, but they were described as being manufactured by Robey, Taplin and Company. Taplin had overstretched himself financially, and, on 25 May 1862, he was declared bankrupt. From this point, Taplin appeared to continue his work as a practising doctor. He died, in Bridlington, in 1910.

In July 1862 an advertisement appeared in the *Stamford Mercury* that Wilkinson, a Hull auctioneer, will sell by auction to:

> ENGINEERS, IRONFOUNDERS, AGRICULTURISTS, SMITHS, and Others at the Patent Crank and Traction Engine Works of Messrs, Taplin and Co., High Street, Lincoln, (a short distance from the Great Northern and Midland Railway Stations and adjoining the River Witham,) on Monday, Tuesday, Wednesday, and Thursday, the 7th, 8th, 9th, and 10th of July, without reserve, the whole of the valuable and modern WORKING PLANT, costly ENGINEER'S TOOLS, STOCK-IN-TRADE, &c, new within 18 months, and principally

from the works of Messrs. Smith, Beacock and Tannett, Woodhead, Scrives, and Holdsworth, of Leeds, and other eminent makers.

The sale details are of considerable interest because they show that Taplin had invested in the very latest machine tools and the detailed listing of tools and materials give an idea as to how a foundry in Lincoln at this time would have been equipped. They included Naylor's patent 10 cwt steam hammer, by the Kirkstall Forge Company; a powerful double-ended punching and shearing machine, punches and shears; Dray's patent 26 horse-power multi-tubular Cornish boiler, with mountings complete; two Schieles's patent noiseless blast fans; portable forges, with double-blast bellows; 120 feet of bright wrought-iron shafting; Whitworth's stocks, taps, and dies; smiths' tools; vices, anvils, ratchet braces, etc.; about 50 tons of rod, bar, and plate iron; 20 tons of pig iron: cast and shear steel; new brass castings; engine and boiler mountings and much else. There were also two completed 12 horse-power traction engines, and partly-assembled smaller traction and portable engines.

Although Taplin and Lee's enterprise lasted only two years, it played an important part in Lincoln's engineering history. Edward Clarke, who in 1859 had a forge in Hungate, was possibly influenced by Lee's invention and patented a process for crank manufacture in 1872. By 1874, he had established Clarke's Crank Works on Coultham Street, which is examined in the next chapter. Lincoln since then has excelled in crank manufacture, with cranks produced in the city still being used in aircraft engines. Taplin and Lee had also produced technically more advanced traction engine designs, which were to be incorporated into Robey's engines. While they may have tried to expand their business too rapidly, the major contributory factor to the failure of Taplin's company was the restriction that had been placed on steam locomotion by the 1861 Highways Act. This had virtually killed the great opportunities that were expected to be created by the introduction of road steam locomotion.

Advertisement from *Bell's Weekly Messenger*, October 1861. This shows the full range of Taplin & Lee's engines. Top: 16/12 hp engines for road haulage and ploughing. Centre: The 8hp engine for general farm work, which was steered using a horse at the front. Bottom: The 8hp portable steam engine.

CLARKE'S CRANK & FORGE COMPANY

Andrew Walker

In 1861, in a newspaper report relating to a railway accident at Greetwell in which his nephew, John Clarke, a millwright of Horncastle was killed, Edward Clarke was described as a blacksmith. Two years earlier, Norfolk-born Edward Clarke had established a forge at 3 Hungate. Initially, Clarke's business was based upon the manufacture of agricultural equipment. However, he soon started specialising in the production of crankshafts for steam engines. By 1864, he had property in Canwick Road as well as his Hungate address. In 1871, he was living at 28 Canwick Road and his business premises were nearby, on Coultham Street, (now the eastern part of Kesteven Street).

Clarke took out a patent in 1872 relating to a hydraulic crank-bending machine. The patented device took a bar of iron at a yellow heat, or red-hot steel, and placed it on a die. One hydraulic ram pressed down on the middle of the bar and two others applied pressure at both ends of the bar, pushing it into the required shape. The process took between six and eight minutes, with movement taking place slowly and steadily, thus preventing the internal structure of the iron or steel from being compromised by repeated hammering. It replaced the need for a smith and two strikers to take up to three hours to produce an equivalent crank – of an inferior quality – from a 3.5-inch iron bar. As a result of this invention, a large number of British firms discovered that they could purchase cranks from Clarke's that were cheaper and of a higher quality than could be produced at their own works. Clarke advertised his products extensively, proudly proclaiming that they were manufactured at the 'Patent Crank Works, Lincoln'. The cranks produced by the company included those for locomotives, portable and fixed engines, thrashing machines, pumps and weaving looms.

In 1875, Clarke's Crank Company became a private limited company, providing the capital to extend further. By 1885, the company had invested in three large steam hammers, and a substantial hydraulic forge manufactured by Messrs Fielding and Platt of Gloucester. In an account of that year of a visit of members of the Institution of Mechanical Engineers to the Coultham Street works, it was reported that the visitors saw the forging press manufacture suspension bridge links. The report speculated that this was the only machine in the country that was adapted for this kind of work. The account also noted that the works employed approximately 100 men, on a site which covered just over two acres and connected with the Great Northern and Great Eastern Railways. In the same year as this visit, the company's name was changed to 'Clarke's Crank & Forge Company', reflecting the wider range of products now manufactured by the firm.

Building plans reveal that further development of the company's works continued, particularly between 1912 and 1920. Prior to the First World War, a new smithing workshop was opened in 1912, and a loading shop and mess room were built in 1913. During the war, substantial growth in production took place, particularly of marine crankshafts. This led to further building work, including roofing over the forge and railway sidings, together with the addition of new 'conveniences', possibly in part to accommodate the needs of the new female munition workers employed at the firm. By May 1915, 25 per cent of Clarke's workforce was either fighting at the front or serving in various departments of the British army. In 1917, the Admiralty provided the company with the necessary funds to invest in extending the forge and machine shop facilities to enable the production of heavy forgings for ships.

Following the First World War, in a difficult market, the company entered a combine with other British engineering companies, called the Agricultural and General Engineers (AGE), which remained in place until 1932. Formed in 1919, AGE was a holding company that combined five British engineering companies: Aveling & Porter, E. H. Bentall, Blackstone, Richard Garrett and J. & F. Howard. Nine other companies were acquired in 1920, including Clarke's Crank & Forge Company (hereafter Clarke's). The aim was to unite these machinery businesses into one strong combine where rationalisation could take place and efficiency be improved. Unfortunately, the expensive London headquarters offset any benefits gained from the amalgamation of the companies and AGE was wound up in 1932. Clarke's was subsequently revived as an independent business.

The company was chaired by Louis Smith from 1909 until his death at the age of 60 in 1939. For many years, he was one of the two principal shareholders, alongside Montagu Waldo Sibthorp (1848-1929) of Canwick Hall. Born in Grimsby, Smith rose from being an engineering apprentice in Lincoln to becoming a board member not only of Clarke's but also a number of other companies, including Doughty & Richardson Fertilizers. From 1928 until his death he was also Conservative MP for Sheffield's Hallam constituency and was resident of Carlton Scroop Hall, near Grantham. Perhaps in part because of the chairman's city connections, the *Sheffield Daily Telegraph* reported regularly on the company, and in 1929, described it as 'a branch of the Sheffield iron and steel trades'.

The company, like many other long-established Lincoln engineering firms, adopted a family-related recruitment

CLARKE'S CRANK & FORGE CO., Ltd., Lincoln.

Telegraphic Address: "CRANKS, LINCOLN."

BENT CRANKS. BLOCK CRANKS.

FORGINGS, SHAFTS, AXLES,

In IRON or STEEL, for ALL CLASSES of MACHINERY.

Advertisement for Clarke's Crank & Forge Company, December 1889. (*Source: Grace's Guide*).

policy with several generations often employed at the works. The local press regularly featured employees' long service milestones. On 24 November 1939, for example, the *Lincolnshire Echo* reported on the retirement of Jack Ball of Sincil Bank, who had worked for Clarke's for 45 years as a crank turner, having served his apprenticeship with Clayton & Shuttleworth. The paper reported that, looking back over half a century, Mr Ball emphasised the great improvements in workshop conditions. At the beginning of his career, employees were expected to start work at 6 o'clock in the morning and labour for 54 hours in the working week, compared to the 7.30 starts and 47-hour working weeks which were the norm in 1939. He recalled the old gas-lit workshops and the inferior steel used, which was brittle and cracked if touched by water when it was hot. He recollected that there were no overhead electric cranes and all the work had to be lifted with the aid of pulley blocks. Nearly seven years later, on 14 August 1946, the *Lincolnshire Echo* reported on '100 years' service by father and son' at Clarke's. William Perkins of Cross Street retired after more than 54 years of service for the company. His father, James, it was noted, had been employed by the company since soon after its opening in 1859. William Perkins had begun working for the firm in 1891 and recalled the days before workers' compensation was inaugurated when employees who were incapacitated at work spent the rest of their lives on 'parish pay'. He also commented upon many improvements in the workplace, including shorter working hours, paid holidays, and improved lighting and heating. Perhaps in such reports inevitably the focus tended to be on positive recollections. Certainly Clarke's adopted a paternalistic approach towards its employees, with occasional trips days out organised for workers and their families, such as a rail excursion to Drinsey Nook in August 1871.

However, employees at Clarke's, as at other works in the city, from time to time took industrial action, either to protect or improve their working conditions in environments which regularly were marred by serious or occasionally fatal injuries to workers. A dispute at Clarke's in 1886, for instance, related to a proposed 5 per cent reduction in pay as a result of a trade depression. Production was halted owing to strike action and the company attempted to sue five men for breach of contract before a resolution was reached.

The dangers of the workplace at Clarke's, as elsewhere in Lincoln's engineering works, can be gauged from reports of serious injury and occasional fatalities. Injuries were usually caused by pieces of iron hitting workers, often on the legs or feet, with amputations occasionally being required, as was the case in August 1868 when a young man named Richard Redman lost two toes as a result of a large piece of bar iron falling upon his left foot. Fatal accidents were reported in the local press at Clarke's. In 1895, William Smith, aged 38, died having fallen from height; Hildred Eldridge, aged 30, succumbed to a head injury following a fall in January 1913; and, in July 1947, Donald Wells, a 25-year-old forge man lost his life two days after being hit in the abdomen by an iron block. Fatalities at the workplace were rare but, nevertheless, the threat of them was always present until health and safety legislation was significantly improved in the second half of the twentieth century.

During the Second World War, Clarke's, like other Lincoln firms, contributed significantly to the war effort. In the later part of the war, as the *Lincolnshire Echo* reported in its consideration of the city's contribution to the war effort on 13 July 1945, the company's crankshafts were used in the development of 'PLUTO', the pipe-line under the ocean, which carried oil and petrol from Britain over the bed of the English Channel, across France and into Germany.

After the war, in 1948, the company was taken over by Mitchell, Shackleton and Company of Manchester which then merged with Walter Somers of Halesowen in 1963. Finally, Clarke's became part of Folkes plc in 1990. In 2003, Folkes announced the closure of the Coultham Street works, and it was subsequently demolished in 2007. Despite the closure of Clarke's, however, the city's long association with crankshaft manufacture continues. Immediately after the demise of Clarke's on Coultham Street, a new firm emerged in 2003 called Lincoln Crankshaft and Machines. It operates from a base on Beevor Street, on part of the former site of Ruston Bucyrus.

Illustration from *The Engineer* depicting Clarke's duplex oil engine, 1896. (*Source: Grace's Guide*).

DUPLEX OIL ENGINE, BY CLARKE'S CRANK AND FORGE CO.

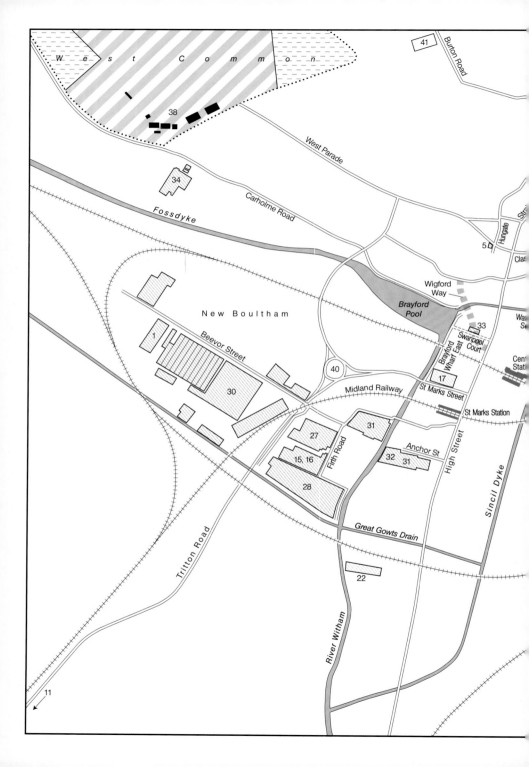

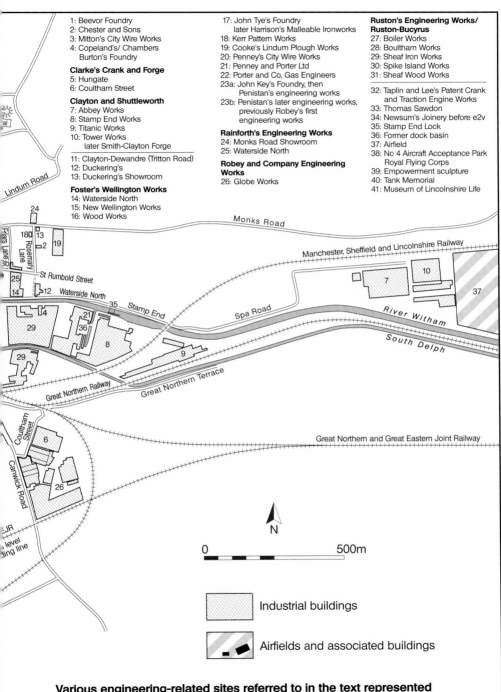

1: Beevor Foundry
2: Chester and Sons
3: Mitton's City Wire Works
4: Copeland's/ Chambers
   Burton's Foundry

Clarke's Crank and Forge
5: Hungate
6: Coultham Street

Clayton and Shuttleworth
7: Abbey Works
8: Stamp End Works
9: Titanic Works
10: Tower Works
    later Smith-Clayton Forge

11: Clayton-Dewandre (Tritton Road)
12: Duckering's
13: Duckering's Showroom

Foster's Wellington Works
14: Waterside North
15: New Wellington Works
16: Wood Works

17: John Tye's Foundry
    later Harrison's Malleable Ironworks
18: Kerr Pattern Works
19: Cooke's Lindum Plough Works
20: Penney's City Wire Works
21: Penney and Porter Ltd
22: Porter and Co, Gas Engineers
23a: John Key's Foundry, then
     Penistan's engineering works
23b: Penistan's later engineering works,
     previously Robey's first
     engineering works

Rainforth's Engineering Works
24: Monks Road Showroom
25: Waterside North

Robey and Company Engineering Works
26: Globe Works

Ruston's Engineering Works/ Ruston-Bucyrus
27: Boiler Works
28: Boultham Works
29: Sheaf Iron Works
30: Spike Island Works
31: Sheaf Wood Works

32: Taplin and Lee's Patent Crank
    and Traction Engine Works
33: Thomas Sawdon
34: Newsum's Joinery before e2v
35: Stamp End Lock
36: Former dock basin
37: Airfield
38: No 4 Aircraft Acceptance Park
    Royal Flying Corps
39: Empowerment sculpture
40: Tank Memorial
41: Museum of Lincolnshire Life

Industrial buildings

Airfields and associated buildings

Various engineering-related sites referred to in the text represented on a modern street map of Lincoln. (Drawn by Dave Watt).

John Thomas Brown Porter and the Gowts Bridge Foundry

Nicholas Moore

In mid-nineteenth-century Lincoln many people who had no obvious background in engineering became involved, often in a speculative way, in engineering enterprises. One such person was John Thomas Brown Porter (1825-76). He first appeared in Lincoln in the 1840s as an insurance salesman, associated with the Lincoln and Lindsey Bank. Then, in 1847, he became active in the movement in Lincoln to limit the hours of shop workers. This was an organisation under the chairmanship of the Hon. Alexander Leslie Melville of Branston Hall. Porter paid for the publication of George Boole's lecture on *The Right Use of Leisure,* which was delivered in 1847. In *White's Directory* of 1856 Porter was mentioned as 'a commission agent' in Lincoln's Cornhill, who lived on Canwick Road. It was shortly after this that advertisements appeared in the *Stamford Mercury* and in many other regional newspapers, indicating that Porter was acting as an agent for George Bower, who had patented 'The National Coal-Gas Apparatus'. This was for use in 'Private Residences, Farm Buildings, Churches, Chapels, Railway Stations, Workshops, Ships etc., and for Exportation'.

George Bower was the Caistor-born owner of the Vulcan Foundry in St Neots in Huntingdonshire. This was a general foundry, but Bower had perfected his National Gas Apparatus by 1851. He began to specialise in the production of larger gasholders and the associated equipment needed for town and city gas production undertakings. He was also involved in the production of pumps and other equipment for waterworks. Much of his production was being exported. In June 1855, he received a patent for his National Coal Gas Apparatus. This proved popular for the landed classes in their country houses and for use on their estates.

The apparatus was stated to be of simple construction, consisting of a furnace and retort portion, the combined apparatus, forming one vessel with the hydraulic-main condenser, scrubber, and purifier, and a gasholder. The apparatus came in four sizes for either 10, 20, 35 or 50 gaslights.

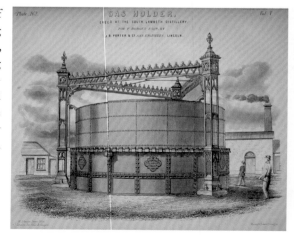

Gas holder supplied to the South Lambeth Distillery by J. T. B. Porter & Co., Gas Engineers in 1860, as illustrated in Practical Engineer of that year. (Source: Grace's Guide).

Apparatus for the production of gas on board a ship. Patented by Porter, 1872. (*Source: Grace's Guide*).

The great difficulties in manufacturing gas on a small scale were claimed to have been overcome. Bower appears to have made the decision to concentrate on his larger schemes. By November 1857 he had sold his general ironmongery business in St Neots and J. T. B. Porter was described as the 'Licensee and Wholesale Agent' for the National Coal Gas apparatus. Presumably Bower was manufacturing the apparatus for Porter. Initially Bower was very successful with his new venture, but he lost money on a large scheme to provide gas lighting for Rio de Janeiro and in 1887 he filed for bankruptcy.

Porter presumably purchased the manufacturing rights to the National Coal Gas apparatus, as in 1859 he described himself as 'Proprietor and Manufacturer'. He developed and manufactured his own gas apparatus, which he advertised from 1860 as the 'Universal Gas Apparatus'. This was developed for the smallest houses, farmsteads and business premises. Porter's apparatus was smaller than that manufactured under the auspices of the National Coal Gas and portable. In 1862, he received backing from Alexander Leslie Melville, who chaired the short-lived Midland Gas Company, which Porter served as engineer. It was probably around 1860 that Porter started manufacturing in Lincoln. He acquired the former tannery buildings at the west end of modern Peel Street, south of Little Gowts Drain, and next to the River Witham. This became known as the Gowts Bridge Works. Padley's map of 1842 shows that the site was approached by a tree-lined lane from the High Street. (Peel Street was extended to the works in 1901.) He now started to manufacture some larger gas installations. In October 1860 he had supplied a gasholder for the South Lambeth Distillery of F. Hodges.

The manufacture of the gas apparatus was not without its hazards. The *Lincolnshire Chronicle* on 24 February 1860 reported:

> Accident to a Citizen in France. —We are sorry to announce that Mr. J. T. B. Porter, commission agent of this city, and proprietor of the patent for the National Coal Gas Apparatus, has met with an accident of a serious nature, near Paris. Last week, he was engaged with some engineers making a series of gas experiments, when an explosion took place, and Mr. Porter was badly burnt about the face, his eyebrows and whiskers being singed off. Inflammation of the eyes supervened.

Porter was successful in selling his apparatus across Britain, including as far afield as north-east Scotland, where James Alexander was his agent in Elgin. The Lincoln architect, Henry Goddard was also enthusiastic about the apparatus. He wrote a letter of recommendation noting that he had constructed a new hunting stables for Lord Henry Bentinck, a mile from Lincoln (off Monks Lane) and had installed the apparatus far more cheaply than the supply from the Lincoln Gas Company.

Porter displayed the gas apparatus alongside the major Lincoln engineering companies at the Royal Agricultural Society's annual exhibitions and the leading county agricultural shows. He won many awards at these shows. In 1862 he hired a stand at the International Exhibition in London, taking out a full page advertisement in the popular guide to the exhibition. It was stated that during this period, when he was employing 20 men at the foundry, he had produced about 600 sets of the gas apparatus, some of which had been sold to country houses, including Holkham Hall in Norfolk, Tyntesfield in Somerset and Fell Foot in Cumberland and, rather nearer to home, sales were made to the Earl of Yarborough at Brocklesby Hall. He also exported some of the gas apparatus across Europe. Porter opened a London office first at 1, Westminster Chambers, London, S.W. and from 1861 at 7 John Street, Adelphi.

A photograph of c. 1900 of the much-used Montague Street footbridge built by J.T.B. Porter & Co. over the River Witham in 1878. According to the mayor, William Cottingham, speaking at its opening in July 1878, to those 'employed at the great foundries the bridge would undoubtedly prove a great boon.' *(Courtesy of the John Wilson Collection, Saxilby History Group).*

In 1872 Porter took out a patent for a gas plant that could be fitted into ships for lighting. His apparatus was used in the SS 'Celtic', an ocean liner built for the White Star Line by shipbuilders Harland and Wolff of Belfast. This was only the second ship in the world to be fitted with such gas-making plant. In 1879, three years after Porter's death, the company J. T. B. Porter and Co., Gas and Civil Engineers was dissolved and continued to trade as Porter and Co. There were some orders for larger gasworks as at Wallingford in 1875 and at Elgin, where in 1883 a new gasholder was constructed capable of containing 50,000 cubic feet of gas, at the cost of £2300.

By the 1880s demand for new gas lighting units for country houses was disappearing. Both acetylene and petrol/air units, which took up less space, needed minimal supervision, and did not require coal storage, started to appear as well as the introduction of electric lighting. Porter and Co. continued to produce and maintain gas fixtures and fittings, and cast lamp-standards, a small number of surviving examples of which can still be seen in the city, for instance, outside the Methodist Church on Bailgate, Wordsworth Street, St Paul's Lane, and on the corner of Spring Hill, Hungate and Michaelgate. Arthur Ward's chapter examines Lincoln manufacturers' production of the city's street furniture. Porter and Co. now started to undertake more general foundry work. This included structural ironwork for bridges and for roofs. Most impressive is the Hibaldstow Bridge over the River Ancholme which was commissioned by the architect Alfred Atkinson in 1889. An iron footbridge by Porter and Co. of 1878 spans the River Witham at the end of Montague Street. Other examples in Lincoln of the company's castings include stanchions of 1891 for the eastern mill of Doughty's Oil Mill and the cast ironwork for the roof of the Drill Hall (1890) as well as street furniture, such as the railing posts on Motherby Hill and pavement gulley covers in several streets.

By the start of the twentieth century the firm was clearly in decline from having been one of the most active and successful gas engineers in the country. It tried to diversify into acetylene lighting and providing acetylene welding to survive. In 1910 much of the foundry was demolished when Peel Street was extended, but the 1922 Ordnance Survey Map shows that a building facing the River Witham was retained. Amalgamation with the firm of Penney's took place by 1919 when Penney & Porter was formed. However, advertisements for Porter and Co. welding services continued until about March 1923, after which Porter and Co. appears to have been fully merged with Penney & Porter. The Porter side of the Penney & Porter business continued to make castings for gasworks for several years. Later, it worked with British Oxygen Company and made vacuum tanks for Clayton Dewandre between the wars.

W. Rainforth & Sons

Adam Cartwright

It is not surprising that Rainforth's is one of the lesser-known Lincoln engineering firms; it was never one of the biggest concerns and the business closed well over 60 years ago. But behind the relative obscurity is a firm whose workforce and leaders showed remarkable adaptability and resilience to cope with market changes, moving through 130 years from river transport via iron founding and agricultural engineering to commercial vehicle body building.

William Rainforth senior, who began the business, came to Lincoln from Gainsborough in 1837, setting up as a sailmaker on Brayford Pool. From a slow start, by the 1850s he had built up a wider range of business interests, including rope making, wire working and a small fleet of barges and keels, serving Sleaford, Horncastle, Gainsborough and Hull. He took his eldest son William into partnership in 1869 (followed by younger son Henry in 1877), establishing the trading name 'Rainforth & Sons', which lasted until the business closed.

By about 1870, Rainforth's had a workforce of around 65 and had taken over a foundry in St Rumbold Street, earlier occupied by Michael Penistan, patriotically renaming it the Britannia Iron Works. From the firm's wire-working experience Rainforth's was able to diversify into corn screens, which sieved out mud and husks from harvested corn, patenting its model in 1870, followed by more new products, including cast-iron benches, drain covers, railings and other street furniture – some of which can still be seen around Lincoln to this day – seed drills, sheep dipping equipment and garden barrows.

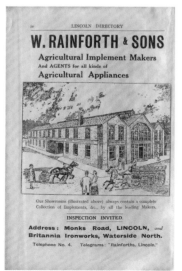

Both William junior, and his brother Henry, led Rainforth's export drive, which by the 1880s was taking the firm's products worldwide, from New Zealand to other countries including Chile, Russia and India. The firm remained much smaller than its Lincoln rivals, the St Rumbold Street site being hemmed in by housing and other property, but in 1887 Rainforth's opened an impressive new showroom and warehouse. This was the Agricultural Hall, on Monks Road, with huge glass windows to show off Rainforth's range more effectively. This now included carts and wagons. No doubt with great relief, in 1900 Rainforth's left St Rumbold Street for foundry and mill premises on Waterside North,

Rainforth's advertisement taken from J.W. Ruddock's *Directory of the City of Lincoln*, 1913, showing the company's Monks Road showrooms, which were opened in 1887. (*Source: Adam Cartwright Collection*).

Rainforth railings on Greestone Terrace.
(Adam Cartwright, 2008).

previously owned by William Foster & Co, for which it paid £4100. The firm retained a boatyard presence on Brayford Pool until the 1930s, however.

Unlike many of his contemporaries, William Rainforth was not active in politics, but he became a sheriff and a magistrate for the city, and was a committed temperance enthusiast. He died in 1893, aged 76, leaving his sons in charge of the business. Henry became a very successful engineer, patenting new products including the Rainforth sack lifter, but a more 'low-tech' product was also selling increasingly well: the humble cart, some of which have proved so durable that they can still be seen to this day.

After the First World War – during which Rainforth's provided its share of wartime work – the business started to lose its way. William junior retired and later died in 1924, aged 78, and Henry took little further part in the business thereafter (he died at the considerable age of 96 in 1946). The next generation went on to varied careers, none of them in the business, such as Henry's son John, who became a specialist at Lincoln County Hospital; and Guy, who was an auctioneer and the son of William and his wife Elizabeth, the daughter of prominent Lincoln architect Pearson Bellamy. Guy died of pneumonia at Rouen in the First World War.

Rainforth drain covering, Ripon Street, 2008. *(Adam Cartwright).*

In 1924 the business was incorporated as W. Rainforth & Sons Ltd, with share capital of £25,000. Managers from outside the family were appointed, probably accounting for a significant change in direction into commercial vehicle body fitting and building. Of course, Rainforth's workforce already had woodworking skills from the large number of carts they had turned out, and with early vehicle bodies featuring mostly wooden construction, the move was logical. Both Lincoln Corporation and Lincolnshire Road Car were major customers for Rainforth's in the late 1920s and 1930s, as were a number of smaller local bus and lorry companies. Particular highlights were two high-specification bespoke and dramatically-styled coaches for Lincolnshire Road Car in 1933.

Like many other manufacturers, Rainforth's was in deep financial trouble by this time, and in May 1933 the company went into liquidation. However, Rainforth's rose from the ashes in 1935 when two former employees, Sid Thorne and Joseph Carrott, went into partnership to buy what remained of the business. Both were experienced coachbuilders: Thorne had spent several years at the Morris car works in Oxford, before becoming works manager at Rainforth's in 1929, whilst Carrott learned his trade at Clayton's, later taking charge of Rainforth's woodworking department. Although the assets of the old business had been sold, they managed to regenerate both the commercial vehicle bodying and the agricultural equipment departments.

Carrott departed in 1938, leaving Thorne to continue as a sole trader. After a few years of post-war recovery in the commercial vehicle business, especially as buses, worn out by hard wartime conditions, were replaced or re-bodied, the early 1950s saw order books drying up and a series of strikes, which encouraged Sid Thorne to retire and sell the business to Ruston's in 1954.

The site of the old, congested St Rumbold Street foundry is now occupied by Lincolnshire Archives Office, and the later Britannia Works on Waterside North is also long demolished, as is the Brayford boatyard. But there are still reminders of Rainforth's, if you know where to look for them. The Monks Road Agricultural Hall, with its 1887 keystone in the roof gable, is now part of Lincoln College, known as the Temple Building. As well as the surviving agricultural equipment, some of which can be seen at the Museum of Lincolnshire Life, there is another relic well worth seeing: a 1931 Bedford WLG 20-seat bus, with a Rainforth body, registered FW 2378, new to local operator Gosling's of Mareham le Fen. It can now be found just a few miles away at the Lincolnshire Aviation Museum at East Kirkby.

Harrison & Co. (Lincoln) Ltd – The Malleable Iron Works

Ken Redmore

Three Lincoln businessmen, Frederick Harrison, Henry Teague and James Birch, established the Malleable Iron Works on Brayford Wharf East at the end of St Mark Street in 1876. The site they purchased was not only close to the city centre but also well placed for transport by water and rail. It had been occupied in quick succession by John Tye's engineering and millwrighting business and then the Midland Iron Works of James Hall & Company. Both firms had made corn grinding mills and portable steam engines and advertised these and other products widely, but neither had lasting success. Tye was declared bankrupt in 1870 and Hall followed the same path five years later. Thus, in taking over the site, Harrison and his colleagues were able to acquire buildings, plant and equipment recently used in a good-sized foundry.

It would appear that not one of the three purchasers had prior practical knowledge of engineering or foundry work. They were an odd assorted trio: Harrison, aged 34, was a solicitor's clerk; Teague was the 53-year-old manager and engineer of the city's waterworks; Birch, the oldest at 62, was a retired builder. It is not known how they came together or how they raised the capital needed for the purchase, but they clearly recognised a business opportunity in the new foundry, for within a short time the ironworks was turning out large numbers of 'whiteheart' malleable castings for engineering firms in the city. So began a business that continued, albeit with changes of location and ownership, right through to the 21st century.

Malleable cast iron, the chief product of the new ironworks, was first created in the United States in the 1820s. Ordinary cast iron is relatively easy to produce by melting and re-casting pig iron from the blast furnace, but castings from this material have both low tensile strength and poor shock resistance. It is well-suited for inspection covers, domestic grates and engine cylinder blocks but not for machinery components where stresses are large and variable. Malleable iron castings overcome these limitations. In the nineteenth century they were made by casting molten pig iron in the usual way in sand moulds on the foundry floor and then, in a second process, heating for a lengthy period in an 'oven' at about 900°C. This annealing process altered the characteristics of the casting: it was now not only hard and tough but also able to withstand the stresses created in, say, an agricultural machine. Unlike cast iron it was also readily machined to

Advertisement for Harrison's products in the *Implement and Machinery Review*, April 1888. (*Source: Ken Redmore Collection*).

a precise shape. When fractured the newly-exposed surfaces were a very pale colour, hence the term 'whiteheart'.

Harrison, Teague and Birch found a ready local market for malleable iron castings. At least two of the large engineering firms in the city, Clayton & Shuttleworth and Robey, could not make the range of strong castings they needed for the manufacture of steam engines, threshing machines and other agricultural machinery. The new foundry was undoubtedly successful: orders for castings soon came from agricultural machine makers throughout Lincolnshire and further afield. The capacity of the foundry was doubled in 1882 when William Spencer's wood yard to the north of the site was purchased. The enlarged site, now almost one acre (0.4Ha) in area, was developed to contain two foundries with travelling crane, two workshops, a blacksmith's shop with stabling, a pattern shop and stores, and a weighbridge. There was also a large house on site for the foreman and his family.

Demand for castings continued to grow and by the end of the century it was apparent that, despite the recent enlargement, the site no longer had the capacity to handle all the business coming the foundry's way. There was a second problem: numerous complaints were being made to the City Council by tradesmen and householders about the 'enormous quantity of black smoke' issuing from the foundry. The 'poor people of St Mark's' could not hang their washing out and passengers using the nearby Midland Station complained that they were 'simply suffocated'.

The firm found a solution to these problems in 1902 when they acquired a 'green field site' of 3 acres on the edge of North Hykeham alongside the Lincoln-Nottingham railway line. Within six years the new foundry's buildings covered half the site and the workforce had grown to more than one hundred. The North Hykeham site had very quickly become the main manufacturing base for the company and, in 1923, the Brayford Wharf site was put up for sale. Unfortunately this was a time of recession and no commercial or industrial firm was prepared to pay an acceptable price for this 'most eligibly situated property'. Eventually the site completely changed its use to become the Lincoln Corporation bus depot; today it is covered by a multi-storey student hall of residence.

At the new foundry in North Hykeham large-scale plant was installed and the market for castings widened considerably. Agricultural machinery continued to be important but the firm also made components by the thousand for railway companies. The burgeoning motor car industry demanded malleable castings too, and soon the company had contracts with manufacturers such as Austin, Triumph, Vauxhall, and Leyland in the West Midlands.

Inevitably the ownership and management of the firm changed over the years. Two of the original investors, Teague and Birch, left the partnership in 1883 and the firm came under the sole ownership of Harrison. In December 1904 the firm was incorporated and registered as Harrison & Co. (Lincoln) Ltd. Frederick Harrison himself died in 1910 – by then a JP and widely respected figure in the city – but the firm continued under his name until bought out by Leys Malleable Castings Ltd of Derby, a large and long-established business, in 1938.

Under the changed ownership there was a far-reaching investment in new equipment and machinery. For the next 30 years the British motor industry was the principal customer of the foundry and it is a tribute to the company's resilience and versatility that it survived the demise of British car making in the 1970s, albeit with staff reductions and decline in profit.

There were substantial changes in 1980 when the Georg Fischer Group, a Swiss company, assumed ownership. After an investment in new plant at a cost of £30 million, the company's export market – principally with European car makers – grew considerably but could not be sustained. A final change in ownership occurred in 2004 when the foundry was sold to the Meade Corporation and renamed Lincoln Castings. This survived for only two years and production finally ceased on the Hykeham site in December 2006. The foundry site is now a

The company's band, comprising workers from both the Lincoln and North Hykeham sites, 1911. The band regularly performed in Lincoln, often occupying the Arboretum bandstand, and winning prizes at contests, such as at Mansfield in July 1911. (*Source: Ken Redmore Collection*).

large housing estate with street names such as Crucible Close, Forge Way and Furnace Close, providing a permanent reminder of the significance of 'The Malleable' to Lincoln and North Hykeham.

(For a detailed account of 'The Malleable' at North Hykeham, see Norman Tate's chapter in *Ploughs, Chaff Cutters and Steam Engines*, SLHA, 2007.)

The Junxion student hall of residence now occupies the former site of Harrison's Malleable Iron Works in the city. (*Andrew Walker*).

Local Street Furniture Made in Lincoln

Arthur Ward

Street furniture constitutes some of the last tangible evidence remaining in the townscape to remind us of our past in terms of examples of Victorian and Edwardian engineering. Items of street furniture include street-name plates, footpath rainwater channels, gratings, inspection covers, railings, lamp posts, bollards and other metal objects that adorn footpaths and highways. Although these survivals are often small and overlooked, they carry the names of several of Lincoln's historic engineering companies. The city, responding to national legislation, notably from the mid-nineteenth century onwards, to address the health, wellbeing and social needs of its expanding population, undertook schemes, firstly, to cleanse, pave and light its streets and, secondly, to deal with its sanitation problems. These measures were essential for an expanding industrial, commercial and residential city.

It should be noted that many of these items bear witness to local style and design, something lacking through later compliance with standardisation based on regulations applied nationwide. These important street furniture items have been vulnerable to change through lack of appreciation of their intrinsic 'local' heritage value as well as neglectful approaches to maintenance and, even in some instances, theft and sale as scrap metal.

Some of the most numerous items of street furniture are those naming streets, terraces and individual dwellings – mainly 'villas' – as well as the small-cast plates indicating house numbers. Early street names in the form of stencilled lettering are still visible on Michaelgate, Castle Hill and Steep Hill, though now supplemented by later Victorian name plates. Francis Hill, in *Victorian Lincoln*, gave an interesting insight into the naming of streets, conducted by the City's Lighting and Paving Commission. The names adopted included Lindum Road (previously known as New Road), Bailgate, Steep Hill and, for the new roads to the village of Canwick, names such as Canwick Road and Melville Street. More widespread house numbering also took place under the authority of the Commission during the 1830s and 1840s.

The Victorian signs we see today are of a standardised design in sand-cast iron, and each one was made to suit the required street name. Individual raised black-painted letters were set within a profiled white-painted frame. Looking along the lower edge of the frame, centrally, you will see 'DUCKERING LINCOLN' in small raised letters. Over 200 of these name plates still exist and can be seen on streets from Newport to Boundary Street, east along Monks Road, and throughout the Carholme Ward, to the west. Their distribution marks the expansion of the city's residential areas up to the First World War through mainly terraced housing, though a few do adorn later inter-war streets. Sadly, many have been removed because of deterioration of the casting and lack of maintenance, and others through replacement with standard, pressed-metal signs.

Charles Duckering, a native of Retford, came to Lincoln in 1845 and formed the partnership Burton & Duckering, initially located on Waterside South. It was not until 1966 that their showroom trading as 'Duckering's Hardware Ltd.' closed on Monks Road. Mark Duckering's chapter on this company can be found elsewhere in this work. As a local company it does appear to have had a monopoly on serving the building trade with street-name plaques, as well as other items, such as drain grates, inspection covers, and rainwater channels to footpaths. These channels were ingenious hollow, square-section, cast-iron ducts, set into footpaths with a small longitudinal opening in the top to allow cleaning and water ingress from footpaths, with raised chevron 'teds' to avoid slipping, all to carry water from dwelling downpipes to the road gutter, without impeding foot traffic. Several of these rainwater channels carry the name 'DUCKERING', as well as 'M. PEARSON' and 'W. RAINFORTH & SONS'. Many of these have been lost through street-works such as the laying of services or re-surfacing. They have been replaced by open concrete or stone channels, if at all. In the streets can be found rainwater (surface water) gulley covers in the channel – heavy-duty liftable gratings – many bearing the name 'DUCKERING' and, in some instances the emblem of the company – a duck on a ring. Make sure you don't have anything loose in your top pockets when you search for these. How many times as a child did you lose marbles down them?

An interesting group of gratings adorns the pavement south of the cathedral on Minster Yard, covering the road channel. These are again from the Duckering Foundry and have hand holes to allow lifting. It is worth noting here the change of typeface used and stamped into the metalwork.

On the houses themselves – mainly those of terraces – can be seen cast iron rainwater goods: gutters and downpipes; an unusual example being that of the lion's head guttering (originally on Scorer Street), an example of which is now on display – serving its original function on an outbuilding – at the Museum of Lincolnshire Life on Burton Road. Within the front wall of many properties, next to the main door, provision was made for a foot – or a boot-scraper. Sadly, few survive, many missing their metal bars; the stone surrounds empty. It is possible that these were originally supplied by Lincoln companies, such as Duckering's.

In the highway itself, following the implementation of a sewerage scheme, (completed in 1881), can be found access and ventilation covers to the drains. These are mainly of circular design with open lattice work or solid. Many bear the name 'DUCKERING'. Within the property boundaries can be found the conventional rectangular cover to inspection holes – access chambers – either cast or of pressed metal, again bearing names of local foundry owners.

The only remaining item, other than the city's 'conduits', of a visible source of water supply (in this instance from a well) is the hand-pump cover situated in Well Lane. Regrettably, this is not the original, but a fibreglass replica. It is possible that the original casing was made locally.

Gas lighting of the city streets, first introduced in 1791, was significantly extended in 1842. A total of 23 additional lamps were proposed, but only 15 were authorised. It was eventually agreed that they be lit from sunset to sunrise. Urban expansion brought with it the need not only for distribution pipes for the gas but for columns and brackets on buildings to carry gas mantles to provide the lighting source. Gaslight illuminated the city's streets until the advent of electricity following the passing of the Electric Lighting Act in 1882, the eventual obtaining of a licence in 1897, and the building of a local power station. Over time, the gas lighting columns were removed to be replaced with an array of different styles and designs as new regulations and increased lighting levels demanded.

A conscious effort was made in the early 1990s to address the loss of gas lights through an initiative between the City of Lincoln Council and Lincolnshire County Council (Highways), with finance from English Heritage and the National Lottery. This sought to retain and refurbish older columns and brackets and reinstate, with replica columns and brackets where locations were identifiable from the Ordnance Survey maps of the City published in 1888. The issue of providing the required electric lighting was overcome by adopting and adapting the design of the former gas mantle and providing supplementary lighting from higher up on adjacent buildings, where applicable, such as in Bailgate. Today, throughout the 'historic core' these refurbished and replica gas lighting columns can be found, bearing the names of Porter & Co., Duckering, Penney & Porter, as well as Foster. Of note is the 'leaning' lamp post on Steep Hill near to the junction with Danesgate. This now carries the name Foster and a cast profile of the Duke of Wellington's head, the company symbol, as they occupied the Wellington Works at New Boultham. (Andrew Walker's chapter on William Foster & Company can be found elsewhere in this collection). The Beevor Foundry, on Beevor Street, supplied the sand-cast replica columns, recasting from an earlier Foster design of a fluted column and adapting the 'foot' and base to accommodate removable panels, to access the electricity supply. These replica columns bear the foundry name and date of manufacture and include a raised profile of the cathedral's west elevation. All are now painted 'municipal' green. Renovated original columns can be distinguished by their bulbous feet. Electricity is provided to them from adjacent modern supply pillars. The replica columns can be found interspersed among the originals. Where there is no room on pavements for columns, the mantles are supported on refurbished and new replica brackets, affixed to buildings.

Sadly, prior to the street-lighting refurbishment scheme taking place, the historic lighting on Motherby Hill was replaced with 'catalogue' columns and mantles, though not before the

Examples of street furniture manufactured by Lincoln firms still visible on the city's streets in 2021. (*All photographs by Arthur Ward*).

original street furniture was recorded by Catherine Wilson for the Society for Lincolnshire History and Archaeology, covering the wide variety of makers of the removed columns. Catherine's article also recorded many of the other items of street furniture that remain today and is an invaluable record of their various designs styles.

Lincoln's topography is recognised through street names like Motherby Hill, as well as Spring Hill, Steep Hill and Greestone Stairs, where can be found handrails to assist one's ascent and descent. Supports for the handrail were made of cast iron by Duckering's, with some still carrying the wooden rail, others replaced by tubular metal scaffold poles. Other locations where handrails can be found include footpaths from Yarborough Road leading down to streets in Carholme Ward.

Many of the city's dwelling-house boundary railings were removed for the 'war effort'. However, some examples of locally-forged or cast Edwardian, Victorian (and earlier, perhaps blacksmith-made) railings still adorn front boundary walls of early properties in the 'uphill' area of the city. In areas of terraced housing, including on Monks Road and adjoining streets, several houses retain their original railings and hand-gates, as on Arboretum Avenue. As part of a street enhancement scheme along both Winn Street and Monks Road, a stretch of walling, railings and gates was reinstated, taking a cast from original railings and gates. This work was undertaken by the City of Lincoln Council's Housing Department, and is described by Frank Hanson, in The Survey of Lincoln's earlier work, *Monks Road: Lincoln's East End Through Time*.

As part of the highway enhancement scheme around Newport Arch – the Roman North Gate into the city – street bollards were introduced to stop traffic encroachment onto the footpaths. These replicate earlier designs and were again produced by the Beevor Foundry in Lincoln.

Examples of contemporary design are worth a brief mention as they complement not only the retained local examples, but also that of the street scene. Examples include the 'drawbridge' outside the West Gate of the Castle. This structure was designed, fabricated and erected by Renshaw & Milner, Claypole, to complement the re-opening of the West Gate itself in 1993. On Steep Hill, in the vicinity of the 'leaning' lamp post (a Foster design) and the replaced handrailing, is a 'modern' bench – The Mayor's Chair' – designed and built by Richard Bett and the Hall Farm Team at Harpswell. The wall to the rear was restored by Lipton and Son. This addition of 2010 together with the handrails, forms a complementary group of old and new 'engineering' street furniture. As a comparison, the railings to the Lindum Road boundary to the Usher Gallery resulted from a competition – 'Forging Links' – and were designed by the Glaswegian metalworker and sculptor, John Creed.

It is not possible to identify where all the examples of locally-made 'metal' street furniture products can be found, nor to ascertain if they were manufactured by 'local' companies, but it should be noted that many are likely to disappear for a variety reasons and actions, or inaction, as already mentioned. Their existence should be identified, recorded, and where possible, given legal status (supported in guidance by *Historic England: Street Furniture: Listing Selection Guide*, 2017), before our unique streetscape loses its character. Street furniture in one area of the city – Wigford – was surveyed in 2004 by John Herridge, the City of Lincoln Council Heritage Officer, and items photographed in 2002. This record can be found on The Survey of Lincoln website. This project, and Catherine Wilson's article, show and describe the vast array of designs of street furniture in far more detail than is possible in this short chapter. But best of all, if you can, go out onto the city streets and look for yourself!

Ruston's, c.1900-45:
Planes, Trains, and Automobiles
Abigail Hunt

The story of Ruston's between 1900 and 1945 is one of both success and failure, but ultimately one of diversification beyond meeting the needs of agriculture. Arguably, the company's foresight in recognising upcoming challenges and ability to adapt to the needs of the modern world ensured that it continued as other well-established engineering companies in Lincoln fell into decline and ceased to trade.

By the beginning of the twentieth century the combined output of the engineering companies based in the city of Lincoln far outstripped the production of any other any town in the county. Steam power was still important to global agriculture before 1914 and the export market was significant until after the First World War. Ruston Proctor & Company had a particularly strong sales market in South America. In Bernard Newman's book celebrating Ruston's centenary in 1957, *One Hundred Years of Good Company*, a former worker, who started as an apprentice in 1900, recalled that:

> Our biggest jobs were portable steam engines, on wheels – for driving generating sets, or pumps – any jobs for which power was required. Then we made traction engines, threshing machines, and other agricultural machinery.

A gathering at lunch hour on Thursday 1 February 1918 of workers and officials to celebrate the formal acceptance by the Air Ministry's William Sefton Brancker of the 1000th aeroplane completed on its behalf by the company. The aircraft can be seen in the background. (*Courtesy of the John Wilson Collection, Saxilby History Group*).

It was in the early twentieth century that the company began to diversify its production beyond steam-powered agricultural machinery to include the development and production of oil engines.

The contribution made by Lincoln and its people to the First World War was significant. Whilst the city's engineering industry is most commonly associated with the production of the first tanks, during the First World War Lincoln was also one of the largest aircraft production centres in the world, building one in 14 of all aircraft made in Britain during this period.

Ruston's had taken its first order for 100 aircraft six months before Foster's started working on building the more famous tanks after responding swiftly to the Government's call for a greater diversion of the engineering industry into aeronautical work. Many of the company's sites in the city became dedicated to aspects of aircraft production. The Spike Island Works produced engines, the Boultham Works manufactured aircraft, and the Anchor Street Works focussed upon aviation-related woodworking. Aircraft production in the city during the First World War is examined in more detail in Charles Parker's chapter.

The company also produced other items for the war machine besides the manufacture of over 2500 aircraft, including 8000 Lewis guns, parts and ammunition, 127 submarine engines, 30,000 sea mines, 2000 paravanes, and flying bombs. In the first period of Total War the world had seen the company also produced oil engines that were used to power amongst other facilities and devices munition factories, searchlight batteries, hospitals, trench pumps and tank engines. In 1915 the company built its first internal combustion locomotive, and over

The company's 1000th aeroplane, Sopwith Camel B7380. It was painted to resemble the Egyptian sun god Heru-Behutet on the instructions of Colonel Ruston, who was a keen Egyptologist. (*Courtesy of the John Wilson Collection, Saxilby History Group*).

the next three years many of those it produced were employed in gunpowder factories, where steam engines, understandably, were not used. The company also produced 442 oil engine tractors for Russian agriculture.

By the end of the war whilst women had specific tasks within the company in relation to aircraft production, such as installing and painting textile coverings to the fuselage and wings, they also undertook heavy work including turning shells and forging ingots. Women were not immediately accepted into the workforce and unions were opposed to women being employed to do jobs that, pre-war, were viewed as only appropriate for men, making calls against the recruitment. There was even controversy when women took up some administrative roles. For example, Bernard Newman noted that it was 'almost a sensation when the first female typist was introduced into the offices'.

Generally, British engineering companies did not adapt well when the Government's war contracts ended and their overseas markets disappeared. However, this was not the case for Ruston's. On 11 September 1918, Ruston, Proctor & Co. became Ruston & Hornsby Ltd, after acquiring the Grantham-based firm Richard Hornsby and Sons and the Stockport firm J.E.H. Andrew and Co. Ltd. Richard Hornsby and Sons Ltd was a smaller company than Ruston's, but was highly regarded for the threshing machines and other agricultural machinery they produced, and well known for moving production from steam to oil engines before 1914. It produced a diverse range of products including excavators, cranes, and steam locomotives. Whilst the newly-formed company continued to manufacture traditional agricultural machinery, it also began to produce excavators, Ruston oil engines, Hornsby safety paraffin engines, and a large range of gas engines.

In 1919 Ruston & Hornsby Ltd expanded its interests further and purchased ordinary shares in the Ipswich-based agricultural engineering firm Ransomes, Sims & Jefferies. Peter Dewey has stated that this arrangement was the only successful post-war market share agreement between large British engineering companies. Agricultural engineering, in particular the production of steam engines and threshing machines, was then moved predominantly to Ransomes, though with some manufacture still taking place at the Grantham works. In 1920 the company provided an 'extensive exhibition' that included 'compound traction engines, steam tractors, threshing machines, binders, [and] a baling press' at the Darlington Agricultural Show, but throughout the 1920s the company reduced its traditional agricultural machinery production. It also failed in a new venture to produce the petrol-driven American Wallis Tractor under licence during the 1920s as it could not compete with companies already producing tractors. Whilst the last steam engine was built in 1936, the company recognised that internal combustion engines were the future and that the application of these engines stretched beyond agriculture. This

Ruston-Hornsby cars in production at the Boultham Works, c.1920. (Courtesy of the John Wilson Collection, Saxilby History Group).

led to diversification in terms of the types of engines that were made, including multi-cylinder vertical oil engines for industrial and marine settings, and small petrol and paraffin engines for agricultural, construction, and modern factories. These engines sold in significant numbers and helped Ruston & Hornsby Ltd move out of the agricultural engineering business. In 1930 the controlling interest in Ransomes was sold, and in 1931 the final piece of agricultural machinery, a clover huller, was exported to Riga in Latvia.

Ruston & Hornsby Ltd continued to diversify after aircraft production ceased, most famously moving into the luxury car business in 1919 by building the Ruston-Hornsby car. Three models were built, but they were expensive to produce, did not sell in the volumes required for success, were heavy in comparison to competitors' cars, and could not compete in a market where other engineering firms were mass producing cheap vehicles. This resulted in the venture being short-lived, with an estimated 1300 to 1500 produced between 1919 and 1924, when production ended. The Siemens' works in Lincoln currently own two Ruston-Hornsby cars, one of which is fully restored and has been driven through the city on special occasions.

Newly-built cars outside the Boultham Works, c.1920. Between 1920 and 1925 approximately 1300 Ruston-Hornsby cars were manufactured. (Courtesy of the John Wilson Collection, Saxilby History Group).

Parts of a Ruston engine being lowered onto a barge by a Ruston crane at Brayford Wharf East, 1935. *(Courtesy of the John Wilson Collection, Saxilby History Group).*

Whilst Ruston's had built locomotives during the First World War, it was not until 1931 that Ruston & Hornsby Ltd began to design and manufacture its own oil-engined, narrow-gauge locomotives for mines, quarries, and other industrial settings. This was in a bid to combat economic decline through further diversification. The venture was more successful than the Ruston-Hornsby car and production continued until 1967. Another success was the 1929 agreement with the American Bucyrus Corporation, which resulted in the creation of Ruston Bucyrus Ltd to market excavators across much of the world, and helped them re-enter the export market. The story of Ruston Bucyrus is told in a later chapter by Derek Broughton. In another successful partnership Ruston & Hornsby Ltd worked with R.A. Lister & Company Ltd to produce vertical high-speed diesel engines, with each company making specific elements of the engine, until Ruston's was able to design and manufacture its own diesel engines without the need for a partner. During this period the company also acquired a controlling interest in Barford & Perkins Ltd of Peterborough and Aveling & Porter of Rochester, which had already merged as their businesses struggled, and it disposed of the Stockport works that had been acquired in 1919.

There was also diversification that was not linked to engineering during the inter-war period. For example, the company repurposed the woodworking shop to make furniture for a while. Another diversification was Colonel J.S. Ruston's 1919 scheme to build a garden suburb in

Lincoln after being inspired by Ebenezer Howard's Garden Cities idea. He bought 25 acres of land from the Boultham Hall estate and formed the Swanpool Co-operative Housing Society, with a view to creating the Swanpool Garden Suburb on the outskirts of Lincoln. This partially-completed project is examined in more detail in a chapter by Lesley Clarke in The Survey of Lincoln's *Birchwood, Hartsholme and Swanpool* volume.

During the Second World War, just as it had done during the First World War, Ruston's made a significant contribution to the war effort. They produced 400 Matilda tanks before moving to the production of 220 Cavalier tanks, 600 Crusaders, which carried Bren guns, 4000 armoured tractors to tow large guns, and diesel engines for submarines, minesweepers, patrol boats, landing craft, and for auxiliary power on larger naval ships, armoured tractors, and even Churchill's wartime bunker.

The diesel locomotives that Ruston & Hornsby had started building in 1931 were now manufactured as flame-proof locomotives for use in underground munition dumps, coal mines, and quarries. Most notably, it built thousands of diesel engines that were used for a variety of purposes across the continents affected by the war.

The importance of the company to the British war machine cannot be underestimated and certainly was not by the German Luftwaffe, which held maps of British bombing targets, including the Ruston & Hornsby works, at its headquarters in Lubeck. The company's wartime success resulted in a further merger taking place in 1940, this time with Davey, Paxman & Company of Colchester, which was known for its vee-form engines that were used by the British forces during the war. This was a successful enterprise that helped Davey, Paxman & Company, which was struggling at the time.

The first 45 years of the twentieth century were eventful for Ruston's. It managed to thrive when many other British engineering companies were failing owing to economic downturns and highly competitive markets. Its success was achieved by shrewd mergers and partnerships, a worldwide reputation for quality products, and continued diversification and innovation. There were notable failures during the period, such as the Ruston-Hornsby car and the Wallis Tractor, but success dominated as it became known for oil engines, diesel locomotive engines, and excavators. The company made significant contributions to the war efforts during the First and Second World Wars, again showing its flair for good business deals, high-quality engineering, and the ability to innovate to meet the needs of the British Government and the armed forces. Whilst other periods of the company's history are dominated by steam or gas engines this period is a tale of planes, trains, and automobiles.

Aircraft Production in the First World War

Charles Parker

At the outbreak of the First World War, major engineering companies were faced with several conflicting problems. Their export trade was severely affected. Most allied merchant shipping had moved from general trade to food imports and support for the war effort. Exporting goods by sea also carried risk from enemy action, especially from U-Boats. At home, the engineering companies' workforces were reduced by the large number of skilled men who volunteered for the armed forces. At the start of the war, senior staff at the War Office and the Admiralty felt that they could get adequate supplies of arms, ammunition and other equipment from their tradional suppliers, such as Vickers and the Royal Ordnance factories, but the Army's failure to win the Battle of Festubert in May 1915 was blamed on a lack of ammunition and the poor quality of some of the artillery shells supplied. There was an outcry in Parliament and the bad press that resulted led to the formation of the Ministry of Munitions later that month, overseen by David Lloyd George.

The new ministry moved quickly to involve private industry in the war effort, and three Lincoln companies received contracts to build aircraft designed by other well-known manufacturers. To ensure rapid and uninterrupted production, the Ministry controlled the supply of raw materials and sent experienced aircraft inspectors into the factories to oversee the work. The shortage of time-served craftsmen, and the increased workload, led to the recruitment of female labour, which proved essential for the war effort. Between late 1915 and 1919, Lincoln became one of the largest centres of aircraft production in the world. Men provided the traditional skills of metal working and woodworking while women sewed the linen coverings of the wings and fuselages. Female workers also painted the aircraft and 'doped' them, applying aircraft dope to the fabric-covered aeroplanes, which was a waterproofing lacquer that was highly flammable and dangerous to use. Women were also employed for various semi-skilled jobs such as crane driving, turning and working in the mould shops.

Ruston, Proctor & Co. Ltd was the first Lincoln company to receive contracts to build BE2 biplanes, designed by the Royal Aircraft Factory at Farnborough, and these were followed by several Sopwith designs; the 'One and a Half Strutter', the

Women employees at Robey & Co. working on the production of aircraft wings, c. 1917. (*Courtesy of the John Wilson Collection, Saxilby History Group, and Robey & Co., via Anthony D. Hancock*).

Sopwith Camel and its successor, the Snipe. These were built in a former threshing machine factory at New Boultham which had only just been completed before the war started, but as production ramped up it was progressively extended westwards towards the railway line to Newark. The company also became one of the largest producers of aero engines, producing over 3000 Clerget rotary engines in a new bay at the excavator works at Spike Island. By 1918, Ruston's employed around 3000 men and women on aircraft production. In early 1918, the company completed its one thousandth aircraft and its chairman, Joseph Seward Ruston, obtained permission from the Ministry to paint the aeroplane in a special colour scheme to commemorate the company's achievement. It was used to undertake leaflet drops over the city, urging the public to buy War Bonds, but was subsequently repainted in the standard scheme and delivered to the Royal Flying Corps.

After the war, the company underwent several organisational and ownership changes and today it is a world leader in gas turbine technology. Boultham Works was eventually sold off and it was used by William Sinclair Horticulture Ltd, a garden supplies company, for several years but in recent years it has been acquired for re-development and cleared. Sadly, the name 'Ruston' on the end of the bay facing Tritton Road can no longer be seen as a reminder of the city's contribution to the war effort.

In May 1915, Robey & Co. Ltd was the second Lincoln company to receive orders from the Ministry of Munitions. Such was the pace of aircraft development that the products of its first two contracts were almost obsolete by the time that they were delivered and only small numbers of the Sopwith Gunbus and Maurice Farman Longhorns were completed. However, Robey's was keen to produce examples of its own aircraft and, to that end, Mr James Arthur Peters was employed as a designer, but only two of his types were completed. The first one was a 'scout' or fighter and, once again, by the time it was produced it was too outdated to proceed. The second of Peters' designs was produced to meet an Admiralty requirement for a naval patrol aircraft which could carry a six-pounder recoilless gun. This resulted in a large machine with two gun pods on the upper wing. Two examples of the Robey-

Sopwith Snipe E7370, built by Ruston, Proctor & Co. Ltd seen on the West Common, 1918. (Source: Ray Hooley).

Short 184 Seaplane N9044, built by Robey & Co. Ltd being tested at Calshot, Southampton Water. (*Source: Anthony D. Hancock*).

Peters Fighting Machine were built, but both crashed during testing, fortunately without fatalities. Most aircraft made in Lincoln were assembled and test-flown at the Royal Flying Corps' No. 4 Aircraft Acceptance Park on the West Common but in order to conduct the trials of its own designs more privately, Robey's leased a piece of land at Bracebridge Heath, just south of St John's Hospital. Products comprising the first small contracts were manufactured in an existing building at the back of the Globe Works on Canwick Road, but as production increased the Ministry provided funds for the construction of two large new bays at the north end of the site. Some fifty years later, after the company ceased trading and went into administration, the site was taken over by Jackson Builders' Merchants. These bays became its bathroom, kitchen and plumbing departments and are still in use after more than one hundred years.

While Mr Peters was working on his designs, Robey's was awarded a series of contracts to produce the Short 184 seaplane for the Royal Naval Air Service (RNAS). The company proved to be extremely competent manufacturers and, by the time production ceased, Robey's had produced more than the parent company, Short Brothers. The two-seat Short 184 was a versatile seaplane used in many different theatres of the war; it could drop bombs, torpedoes and flares and it was also used for reconnaissance. They were delivered to Marine Aircraft Acceptance Depots by rail, partly dismantled, and then assembled and test flown by RNAS crews.

Although the West Common was suitable for testing small and lightly-built aircraft, such as the Sopwith Camel, by 1917 its limitations were becoming apparent. It sloped sharply from the east and this was the general approach route for most of the year. Pilots also had to fly over a built-up area, which was not ideal, and it was not suited for the large bombers that Clayton & Shuttleworth began building in 1918. The Royal Flying Corps decided to develop Robey's aerodrome at Bracebridge Heath for both training and test flying, and seven Belfast-truss hangars were built on the east side of London Road with a domestic camp on the opposite side of the road. This site was developed by the A.V. Roe Repair Organisation in the Second World War, and some of these buildings are still in use at the time of writing.

The final company to receive aircraft production contracts was Clayton & Shuttleworth Ltd, based at Stamp End by the River Witham. This had long been the main agricultural engineering company in the county but it was the last in the city to receive aircraft contracts. It began by undertaking sub-contract work for other companies, and then built tail surfaces for small naval airships, which were used for coastal patrol. Contracts were then received to produce Sopwith Triplanes for the RNAS. However, part way through this work a decision was taken to switch to making Sopwith Camels for the Royal Flying Corps. These were all produced in the Titanic Works, which had opened in 1912, east of the main Stamp End Works. The Sopwith Camel flown by Capt. Roy Brown when Manfred von Richthofen, the 'Red Baron', was shot down in April 1918 was built by Clayton & Shuttleworth.

By the early part of 1917, plans were being laid to develop an independent bomber force to strike at enemy industry and not just support the actions on the Western Front. Several large bombers were designed but even the larger engineering concerns did not have the capacity to produce these in their existing premises. The Ministry of Munitions financed the building of a number of National Aircraft Factories, and Clayton & Shuttleworth was asked to manage NAF No. 4, which was built on a new site on the north side of the River Witham, off Monks Road. It was built by Dick, Kerr and Co. and some labour was supplied by prisoners of war who lived in a camp adjacent to the site. This new aircraft factory, the Abbey Works, had machine shops, sub-assembly areas and a large final assembly shop which could build three large bombers side by side. In addition, the welfare facilities were also built to a high standard for both men and women. Tower Works was built next to this with three forging bays to replace the old forges at Stamp End, which were in poor condition. Finally, a flying-off field was laid out to the east. A contract for 50 Handley Page 0/400 bombers was placed in 1917 and the first one was delivered in April 1918.

Ruston Proctor's Excavator Works, Beevor Street, Lincoln. The aeroplane engine bay is the long building next to the railway line. (*Source: Peter Robinson*).

While the Handley Page order was in progress a second contract for twin-engined Vickers Vimy bombers was placed and work began towards the end of 1918. Initially the bombers were flown off to the West Common, but if the war had continued there were plans to build two large assembly sheds at Bracebridge Heath so they would have been delivered in component form and assembled and test flown there. After the end of the war, Clayton & Shuttleworth took the opportunity to buy the site from the Government for £50,000. Sadly, the company struggled in the 1920s and it went into receivership and was progressively broken up, as is discussed in Rob Wheeler's chapter, which explores the history of this company. At the Armistice most contracts were cancelled but production did not cease immediately and deliveries continued into 1919, although at lower rates.

The final totals of aircraft produced during the First World War in Lincoln were:

Ruston Proctor & Co. Ltd:	Robey & Co. Ltd:	Clayton & Shuttleworth Ltd:
200 RAF BE2s;	30 Sopwith 806 Gunbuses;	46 Sopwith Triplanes;
350 Sopwith 1½ Strutters;	17 Maurice Farman Longhorns;	625 Sopwith Camels;
1575 Sopwith Camels;	2 Robey Peters Fighting Machines;	46 Handley Page 0/400s;
525 Sopwith Snipes.	235 Short 184s.	c. 20 Vickers Vimys (some delivered dismantled).

The Decline and Fall of Ruston Bucyrus: A Personal Recollection

Derek Broughton

A memory of Lincoln's High Street is the long-gone Avoiding Line overbridge and its advertising boards, which for many years carried the advertisement 'Ruston Bucyrus cranes and excavators span the world'. And so they did. In its various incarnations, Ruston's existed in Lincoln for 125 years and produced some 40,000 machines in total, used across the world, from Aden to Zanzibar. But is it still an ongoing success story? Surely what was for some time in the second half of the twentieth century the largest plant for the production of excavating machinery in Europe must be still in production and a respected name? Sadly, it is not.

Those who may not be aware of Lincoln's past history perhaps on visiting the city's 'B & Q' store on Beevor Street off Tritton Road may wonder why it is situated close to partially derelict industrial land, but for many there are memories of generations of families working at what was then the Ruston Bucyrus site, and the phalanx of cycles on the Ropewalk at knocking-off time.

The author of this chapter probably bears the dubious distinction of being, in 1999, the last employee to cycle out of the factory gate at knocking-off time. After 30 years employed on the site, and working from the glory days to the end, have left many memories. These recollections, then, are not a definitive history, but a personal memory of how it was seen by one employee.

Ruston Bucyrus was born on 1 January 1930, as a marriage of convenience between Bucyrus Erie USA and Lincoln's Ruston and Hornsby. Bucyrus wanted a presence in the European markets, and Ruston, in the middle of the Great Depression, had a range of excavators which were becoming rapidly obsolescent, and did not have the finances to introduce newly-designed machines or new technology. By the mid-1930s, all the earlier Ruston-designed machines had been phased out, and anglicised versions of US-designed machines were coming off the Lincoln production lines. The manufacture of these new products was in fact relatively easy to implement as the only real alteration was the use of what was then the British standard of Whitworth threads for all nuts and fixings. The main features of the US designs were retained in their entirety, including the use of steel castings for major components. This became a major selling point for the Ruston Bucyrus (RB) range of machines right through until the late 1980s. Whereas all of RB's competitors used a welded steel structure for the machine mainframe, RB, with the exception of the smaller 10RB machine, always used a solid-cast steel bed. This prompted the wisecrack heard more than once – 'It takes one man to bust six [competitor's machines], but six men to bust one Ruston'. The evidence of this is the fact that, for some years, RB was the second biggest user of steel castings in the UK. Right through until the mid-1960s the RB range was entirely 'rope' operated: the engine drove the clutch; the clutch drove the gears; the gears drove another clutch; the clutch drove the winding drum; the drum pulled the rope; and the rope pulled the bucket, lifted the load etc.. 'Rope' is not

A 22RB machine photographed in 1970: almost 10,000 of these machines were built between 1940 and 1990. (*Source: Derek Broughton*).

an exact definition: all riggings were actually steel cables, where the breaking strain could be measured in tens of tons.

So what went wrong? In the 1960s most RB machines were selling well, but by then they were machines with a history. The major seller, the 22RB, had roots going back to the early 1940s. The next largest seller, the 30RB originated in the mid-1950s. During this decade, other machines produced by the company that continued to sell relatively well included the 38RB, which dated back to the late 1940s, and the 54RB, which had begun production in the mid-1940s. Even the largest machine, the 71RB, had been manufactured for at least 10 years in the 1960s. Yes, they were selling well, but the fact still remained that they were all built to a basic design that originated at the turn of the century, based mainly on clutches and gears. By the early to mid-1960s, however, rival manufacturers were embracing a whole new concept. This was hydraulics, a brave new world, and a means of obtaining 'more bang for your buck'. There was no longer a need for an assemblage of sprockets, chains, gears, shafts, and couplings to turn power from the engine to turns of the rope drum. Instead, all that was now needed was a high-pressure oil pump, coupled directly to the engine, a simple control valve arrangement, two high-pressure hoses (flow and return), and a high-pressure motor directly coupled to the winding drum or cylinder.

Another further bonus for the hydraulic drive was the increasing awareness of the dangers of asbestos. Clutches were an irreplaceable component in every drive train of every RB machine, to swing, to move, to lift, and to dig. Each function had a clutch, each

The 3RB, the company's first hydraulic machine. Here, one of these machines is seen on the west side of Lincoln's High Street in 1964. (*Source: Derek Broughton*).

incorporating multiple asbestos blocks, each the approximate size of a paperback novel, and by the very nature of their purpose, each function generated friction. Clutches inevitably produced asbestos dust.

The first real inroad of the hydraulic concept into the excavating machinery market was the 'Backhoe', or 'Backacter'. These became ubiquitous on every building site, where hydraulic cylinders on a long handle connected to a right-angle base boom that pushed the bucket in towards the operator. The concept came from the USA in the early 1960s, and was taken up with great success in Wales by the HY-MAC company, which, in the 20 years following the mid-1960s, sold over 10,000 machines to that design.

And RB's answer? Launched in 1963 was the 3RB. The upper works and front end were modern hydraulics, but, to save money, it used the old 1930s 10RB bottom end and tracks. The design, with the hydraulics, employing Lucas components originally designed for aerospace usage, plus the sheer power of the motors, regularly broke the track-drive train, and, in spite of being described in the sales literature as a quality product designed for long-term reliability, was quietly killed off in 1968, with total sales of just 80.

A lesson learned? Regrettably not. By 1968 control of Ruston Bucyrus was actually firmly in the hands of Bucyrus Erie in the USA, and Lincoln was told to build the solution to the hydraulic problem in the form of the USA-designed 20H and 30H machines. These were new, but with a low-pressure hydraulic system indirectly controlled through an add-on air system, plus a badly under-designed basic structure that led to many major structural failures, it proved to be another disaster. Some rather cruelly claimed that the machines couldn't even climb a kerb.

Once more, RB did not break the five-year production barrier, and after the production of a mere 220 machines in total, another RB tilt at the hydraulic windmill was killed off. This was in spite of an extremely costly rework programme to update earlier machines, and it was the only time in RB's history where it succumbed to the dubious automotive practice at the time of allocating a current serial number to a reworked machine and selling as new.

Quo vadis? The 1972 demise of the 'H' series signalled a long-awaited sea change, in that, concurrent with its UK death, permission was finally given from the USA for RB to spend whatever was necessary to design and develop a machine that not only gave what the UK and European markets wanted in specification and capability, but also met similar requirements for reliability and accessibility. This was accepted as the only way forward following what could only be described as a 'frank' comment in the RB's pitch to the USA for at last permission to create a decent hydraulic. 'Above all except price, reliability in service is essential – this is an area where we failed with the "H" series, and we cannot afford a repetition – good access should be provided to all machinery, and it should not necessitate a contortionist … to access any component'.

There is an old engineering adage – 'if it looks right, it probably is right' – and RB's 'RH' series, over three years in gestation, with the first, the 150RH hitting the market in 1975, it looked the part and was the part. After an early hiatus before the original specification 4-cylinder Ford engine was replaced by a more powerful 6-cylinder Perkins power unit, the construction industry said that RB had finally produced a 'good 'un'.

And yet? The initial sales pitch to the USA defined price as a major factor in any policy decision, and even if the future seemed positive when the decision was taken to embark on the 'RH' series, by the time the range had been also extended to include the larger 220RH, and a rubber-tyre version of the 150RH, the whole project was losing money. The price the market was prepared to pay, even for an excellent machine, was below the price at which RB could make a profit, and so yet again, in 1985, after fulfilling existing orders, RB quietly withdrew from the hydraulic market. The final internal inquest on the project stated 'machines were never built in sufficient quantities to allow economic purchase of bought-out main components'. Whilst the traditional RB rope machines would have an out-purchased component of possibly 25%, hydraulic machines were basically 75% bought-out. Components such as tracks, pumps, motors, and valves were bolted-on to an RB steel frame. With RB components comprising only 25% of the product, inevitably production of spares was also not generating much in the way of income.

So what was left for RB in 1985? By the 1970s, hydraulics systems were also becoming well entrenched in competitors' products in RB's original markets of lattice-boom cranes and excavators. At this stage, RB's machines were being described in the trade press as dinosaurs. A confidential management report as early as the 1970's summed it up perfectly: 'Regrettably it is now recognised by RB management that our customers have been content for too long with old-fashioned features on our rope machines and as a result the world has passed us by'.

This report was actually a preamble to a proposal submitted by RB to the USA to develop the HSC Project, a modern, state-of-the-art hydraulic crane/dragline, which was fully compliant with all UK and continental standards, at a price which the market could stand. However, after consideration, the US parent company vetoed the proposal, and ordered the existing 'RB' range to be tweaked and to soldier on. The 22RB was uprated to the Heavy Duty, the 30 RB became the series 5. The 38RB Series 2 Heavy Duty was uprated, the 71RB series 3 was uprated. Air servo controls became standard to reduce operator fatigue, cab noise insulation became standard as did improved heaters, but under these trimmings there still remained the same designs, 20-plus years old, with the ticking time bomb of asbestos.

The answer? To all the remaining RB employees (now in the lower hundreds rather than the thousands of happier days), it was obvious for some while that something must have been afoot, with spare factory bays vacated, and auctions taking place of component stocks, raw materials, and machine tools. On 1 November1985, Bucyrus America (the controlling interest) disposed of RB to a management buyout. On that day, Ruston Bucyrus ceased to exist.

The subsequent machine manufacture at Lincoln, after the initial few years running out and selling of the traditional RB machines (the author helped to build the last 22RB in 1992) was a time of transition, both in terms of product manufacture, but also with regard to company ethos. Instead of trying to support a long product range, RB transformed through acquisition and innovation into a niche market supplier of specialist long-range hydraulic excavators and high-tech, state-of-the-art, lattice-boom hydraulic cranes. Both of these products seemed to have a bright future. Whilst the product on offer was now very good, twice in the 1990s the prospects for sales through two world recessions were not. Although the company weathered the early-1990s' Far East economic storm, the economic downturn of the late 1990s, plus the fact that the company was now a niche market supplier with cash flow very dependent on machine sales meant that there came a point when, because acceptance of one new machine, and consequent payment, was put back by the customer, the mathematics of cash flow simply did not add up, and there existed no option but go into administration.

Sadly, the hopeful ongoing sale of the company as a going concern to an overseas company, and promise to continue manufacture in Lincoln, became derailed in negotiations at the very last minute. Instead, RB International, as it had become, which had entered administration in July 2000, was bought by the Clarke Chapman Group in December 2000 and a new company, RB Cranes Ltd, was formed. In January 2001, production ceased at the company's Lincoln works, with production transferring to sites in Gainsborough and Retford. Thus, in 2001, the last machine left the Lincoln works and a long and proud history came to an end of what was literally heavy engineering – the final design CH135 crane, was tested to 150 tons. This was a sad end to a company that was a once-mighty engineering empire.

Electronic Manufacture in Lincoln to the 1980s and Beyond

Colin Smith

Electronic component manufacturing began in Lincoln when the valve producer British Thomson Houston, a Midlands-based company, acquired the former Newsum Joinery factory on Carholme Road. The purchase of the site in 1956 was prompted by the development of new silicon semiconductor power device technologies by the company, which was a subsidiary of the Associated Electrical Industries Group. There was an increasing demand for power electronic equipment and so new premises were needed in order to increase its manufacturing capacity. Much restructuring had to be undertaken on the site and initially some of the existing prefabricated bungalows built by Newsum were used for semiconductor production.

A year later, in 1959, the factory became the Valve and Semiconductor Engineering Department of the organisation, which subsequently become known by its parent company's name, Associated Electrical Industries (AEI). In 1960, 750 people were working on the site. However, there were practical difficulties in trying to manufacture valves alongside semiconductors, so in 1964 the valve business was sold to the English Electric Valve Company (EEV). The whole site was bought by EEV, which subsequently rented half of it to AEI for the manufacture of its semiconductors. A partition wall was erected in the factory building between the two manufacturing units.

In the 1960s significant changes occurred in Britain's electrical industries. The government of the time invested substantially in these industries. Equally important was the reorganisation starting at this time of GEC, AEI, and later English Electric, by Arnold Weinstock. GEC acquired AEI in 1967.

AEI's production in Lincoln grew substantially and a new three-storey factory bay was completed in 1975. This doubled its power semiconductor manufacturing capacity and also allowed its small high-frequency microwave semiconductor business to grow.

The AEI new factory extension on Carholme Road, Lincoln in 1975, showing the name of the GEC parent company. (*Photograph reproduced from an AEI Semiconductors publicity booklet, produced by C.V. Middleton and Son*).

By 1981, the works had expanded significantly. In that year, the company Marconi Electronic Devices (MEDL), a part of the GEC organisation, was established with its main base on Doddington Road. This site was developed to cater for the anticipated extra business, especially in integrated circuits. The manufacture of power products continued at the Carholme Road factory for a few years longer.

During the 1980s, MEDL's involvement in electronic component manufacture looked set to have a rosy future. However, after a few years of good growth, the company's markets in aerospace, defence, automotives and telecommunications became much more competitive and so MEDL reduced its range of products, concentrating on fewer but more profitable types. MEDL then became a victim of the break-up of the GEC organisation.

As part of the split, both MEDL's Power and Microwave divisions survived and prospered in Lincoln, although under different ownerships. As well as Power and Microwave, the other Lincoln electronics company inside GEC, which remained in Lincoln after the re-organisation, was EEV, where electronic valves were produced for industrial sectors including medicine, avionics, radar and broadcasting.

The power semiconductor business concentrated increasingly on higher-power products. Important applications were typically for speed control for high speed trains, for example the French TGV. Another important use was control of electrical power transmission, for example in the Channel Tunnel, which was constructed between 1975 and 1986. This 2000-megawatt system joined the British and French AC power grid networks using a high voltage DC current (HVDC) link. Employing DC current for the link minimised the technical problems of synchronising the two systems and it allowed power to be transferred in either direction. Early in 1982 the company received its biggest ever order for £10 million, mainly for power semiconductors for this project.

The Dynex Factory, Doddington Road, Lincoln in May 2021. (*Colin J. Smith*).

In January 1984, several companies in China were interested in taking a licence from MEDL to manufacture power semiconductors. MEDL chose Chun Shu as a partner, which was located in Beijing, and, after a visit by Chun Shu engineers to Lincoln, and a short period of negotiation, an agreement was made in 1984 to supply technical knowhow and product. This eventually led, in 1988, to a comprehensive £1 million technology and commercial agreement with the Chun Shu Rectifier. All this led to Chun Shu building a copy of the Lincoln Power Division factory in China, although on a much larger scale. Chun Shu's main outlet is in China's fast-growing high speed train network.

In 1990, MEDL changed its name to GEC Plessey Semiconductors and, in 1994, moved all of its power division business from Carholme Road to Doddington Road. A year later, EEV bought the microwave business formerly part of MEDL and so the two companies that had occupied the Carholme Road factory site were combined. EEV now occupied the entire Carholme Road site. In 2002, EEV changed its name to e2v as part of a management buyout. The original Carholme Road site was then closed in 2010 and has since been redeveloped as a housing estate. In 2011, a new e2v centre opened in Sadler Road, off Doddington Road, where microwave high-tech products are designed, developed and manufactured. Teledyne Technologies subsequently acquired e2v, in 2017, and has renamed the company Teledyne e2v.

Meanwhile, at the Doddington Road site, in 2000, GEC Plessey Semiconductors' power semiconductor and silicon-on-sapphire product business was acquired by Dynex Power Inc. of Canada. Eight years later, in August 2008, the Chinese business Zhuzhou CSR Times Electric purchased a 75% share in the company. Dynex's products are applied extensively in the industrial, traction, energy and electric vehicles sectors in markets in Europe, the United States and the Far East.

Lincoln, then, remains an important centre of electronic-related engineering product development and production. As has been the case since the industry's arrival in the city in the late-1950s, its ownership rests with large organisations, now with substantial international interests that will inform the future development of the Lincoln sites.

Footnote: Much of the material for this chapter is drawn from *Medallion,* the internal MEDL newsletters, published between July 1982 and May 1990.

Lincoln's Engineering Heritage

Heather Hughes and Tom Kitchen

This chapter focuses on the various ways in which Lincoln's engineering past has been remembered in the present, an achievement that is due largely to the concerted efforts of individuals and interest groups. We cover various kinds of heritage, from the prominent and obvious to the inconspicuous, intangible and fleeting.

Because of their sheer physical size, the most notable reminder of the city's heavy engineering past are the cavernous former works buildings, especially in the Great Northern Terrace area, along Canwick Road and in Spike Island/New Boultham. William Foster's is the only one of the 'big four' engineering works to have disappeared completely. The significance of the company's site in New Boultham is marked by a plaque at the entrance to Morrison's supermarket on Tritton Road. It pays tribute to the company's managing director, Sir William Tritton, and the role he played in the development of the tank.

Ruston's extant original buildings (there was an unsuccessful attempt to rescue the vast former Boultham works in 2018), as well as those formerly belonging to Robey & Co. and Clayton & Shuttleworth, have mostly been converted to commercial uses. Echoes of the upper-gabled structures of Ruston's Spike Island works have been incorporated into nearby modern buildings along the northern boundary of the B&Q premises on Beevor Street. There are some tangible remains of smaller works, too: Rainforth's on Monks Road and Chester and Sons in Rosemary Lane, for example. Although several of these old structures are on Lincoln's Local List of Buildings and Structures of Importance, none has protected status.

Little remains of the wealthy and influential managing directors' opulent residences. The Lodge of Nathaniel Clayton's Eastcliff House still stands, while the gates to Joseph Ruston's Monks Manor estate on Greetwell Road, originally installed in 1895, were removed to the main entrance of Boultham Park in 1934. The significance of these families can also be appreciated from their burial places. In the old Eastgate Cemetery, a large, intricately carved marble cross marks the burial site of Joseph Ruston and several

A maker's mark: William Foster & Company's Wellington Works memorialised on street furniture. (*Tom Kitchen*).

'Empowerment': a public sculpture spanning the River Witham south of the Waterside Centre. (*Heather Hughes*).

other family members; likewise, the Rainforth Obelisk is a prominent feature in the Canwick Road Old Cemetery.

Street names and built spaces recall the city's engineering heritage, although the largest companies dominate this form of memory-making. Street names include Tritton Road, Foster Close, Robey Street, Shuttleworth Court and Ruston Way. Large sites include the Tritton Road Retail Park. In terms of buildings, Shuttleworth House is one of the tallest in the city, while Ruston House serves as office space for Siemens. One of the largest student residences at the University of Lincoln is The Pavilions on Ruston Way; it is made up of Clayton House, Foster Lodge, Hornsby Mews and Proctor Mews. Clayton Ward and Shuttleworth Ward can be found in the county hospital.

Makers' marks on street furniture act as perpetual advertisements for 'made in Lincoln' brands and recontextualise otherwise banal objects as important heritage ones. One can find the names of Duckering and Rainforth on many maintenance hole covers, and Beevor Foundry on cast-iron bollards, for example in East Bight. Duckering, Rainforth and Porter are marks that feature on cast-iron railings, for example on Motherby Hill, while Porter's mark is proudly displayed on the iron bridge over the River Witham at Stamp End.

Beevor Foundry, Duckering, and Penney & Porter were the three principal manufacturers of the most elaborate statements, street lights. The makers' marks range from modest (simple embossed capitalised letters at the base) to highly decorative. Beevor continued to produce 'heritage' street lamps into the 21st century, indicating a shift in conservation attitudes and aesthetics in the built environment. Much of this locally-produced street furniture is examined in more detail in Arthur Ward's chapter.

Lincoln possesses comparatively little in the way of public sculpture and statuary, yet two substantial examples relate directly to its engineering past. The first, called 'Empowerment', was completed in 2002 and spans the River Witham south of the Waterside Centre. Sponsored by Alstom (now part of Siemens), the sculptor was Stephen Broadbent. His two elongated steel and aluminium abstract figures reach out to each other high above the river, recalling turbine blades.

The second directly references Lincoln's wartime production. The Lincoln Tank Memorial was erected on the Tritton Road roundabout in 2015 to mark Lincoln's claim as the 'birthplace of the tank' one hundred years earlier. The sculpture takes the form of a two-dimensional silhouette of a life-size, Mark 1 tank and is made of corten steel. Michael Credland was the designer. Several two-dimensional silhouetted figures, designed by Robin Wheeldon, surround the tank. They represent members of the workforce at William Foster's, manufacturers of the first tanks. The Lincoln Tank Memorial Group led the fundraising campaign to cover the £90,000 cost. Interpretation was added in 2017, when the whole creation was handed over to Lincoln City Council.

The Museum of Lincolnshire Life (MLL) is an important memory institution in the city, which preserves an original tank and many other artefacts related to Lincoln's engineering heyday. Its tank, 'Daphne', was not actually manufactured in Lincoln, although interpretation added in recent years informs visitors that it was built according to plans drawn in Lincoln. Other war-related objects in its collection include wooden aircraft propellers manufactured

The Lincoln Tank Memorial, Tritton Road roundabout. (*Heather Hughes*).

in the city. The MLL's greater claim to significance, however, lies, as Catherine Wilson has noted, in 'the quantity and quality of its agricultural engineering collections'. Many of its rare and unique objects were manufactured in Lincoln, including a steam traction engine, a horizontal winding engine and a crawler tractor. The Museum has suffered from funding cuts and Lincolnshire County Council's adoption of a 'cultural enterprise model'; it is to be hoped that its vitally important collection survives intact, with adequate support to preserve it.

Siemens' Lincoln factory is the current manifestation of the company that began as Ruston, Proctor & Co., and is still a hub for engineering innovation, in partnership with the University of Lincoln. It has taken on the project of refurbishing two 1920s Ruston cars, including the use of 3D printing for parts no longer obtainable. The cars are on display at various local events. Several important examples of goods manufactured in Lincoln are displayed elsewhere in the UK. For example, the original Mark 1, 'Little Willie', is in the Tank Museum at Bovington in Dorset; the Robey Trust, based in Devon, celebrates machines engineered in Lincoln; and aircraft as well as agricultural machinery manufactured in the city can be seen in the Shuttleworth Collection at Old Warden in Bedfordshire.

There are documentary records of all of the large, and several smaller, Lincoln engineering firms in Lincolnshire Archives, including major collections of Robey & Co., and Ruston & Hornsby. The Archives recently received nearly £100,000 from the National Lottery Heritage Fund to digitise the latter, partly to make the collection more widely available but more pressingly because the quality of many original documents, such as photographic negatives, is rapidly deteriorating. The main Clayton & Shuttleworth collection is at the Museum for English Rural Life at the University of Reading. The Media Archive for Central England, located at the University of Lincoln, contains many moving images of Ruston & Hornsby, which are viewable online. The Lincolnshire Film Archive's holdings include footage of machinery in use in the fields, such as of a steam traction engine now in the MLL.

There have long been active industrial archaeology groups dedicated to preserving the region's industrial heritage. Although their remit has been county wide, they have done much to raise awareness about Lincoln's engineering heritage. The Lincolnshire Local History Society, forerunner of the Society for Lincolnshire History and Archaeology (SLHA), established an Industrial Archaeology Committee in 1964; the SLHA's Industrial Archaeology Group continues as one of its special interest groups, holding an annual conference and producing a variety of publications.

The Industrial Archaeology Group has also organised themed trails, such as on the occasion of its hosting of the Association for Industrial Archaeology Conference in 2009. The Lincoln trail covered many of the sites discussed in this chapter. The city trails marking the RAF's centenary in 2018 also referenced many facets of Lincoln's aviation engineering history, for example the site of the Kerr Pattern Factory on Rosemary Lane, the women's football teams from the aircraft works and the aircraft test site on West Common. Visit Lincoln, the city's destination management organisation, has yet to add an engineering trail to its tourism offer; this remains a neglected theme in the visitor economy.

Engineering has been celebrated in at least two prominent festivals in Lincoln. Spark Engineering Festival, sponsored by local firms, local government and educational institutions, first took place in 2014 in the Cathedral. It included a vast timeline of engineering production in the city and a Foucault pendulum suspended from the Cathedral's roof. The most recent occurred in 2019; it is to be hoped that it will return.

Less directly tied to engineering, it is nevertheless fitting that Lincoln should have hosted the Steampunk Festival since 2009. Organised by the Ministry of Steampunk, it is the biggest event of its kind in Europe. Characterised by shows, market stalls and the participants in 'retrofuturistic' costume, the festival recalls the days of heavy industrial steam power. In keeping with its spirit, many shops decorate their display windows in Steampunk style.

Lincoln's rich engineering heritage is poorly served in terms of online resources. For example, there is only the briefest mention on the Visit Lincoln site and the MLL does not possess an adequate website to showcase its collections. While *Grace's Guide to British Industrial History* includes several pages devoted to Lincoln's former engineering works, local individuals and interest groups have plugged the gaps. For instance, the website 'It's about Lincoln and Lincolnshire', contains many posts on this theme.

Lincoln's engineering heritage is thus in an odd situation. It is valued by individuals and civic associations in the city and elsewhere in the UK. Its artefacts are cared for in numerous important collections, although those *in situ* have been starved of resources. And its potential to draw visitors to Lincoln, though evidenced in successful events, remains largely untapped.

Select Gazetteer of Lincoln-Based Engineering Firms[1]

Name of firm	Dates	Location(s)[2]
Barrett, Thomas	1790s-1820	St Mary's Street
Barrett, Lucy	1820-35	St Mary's Street
Barrett, Robert	1835-38	St Mary's Street
Beevor Foundry	c.1995-2005	Bay 20, Beevor Street
Burton, John	1835-40	Phoenix Foundry, Waterside South
Burton, John & Proctor, James Toyne	1840-42	48 Waterside South
Burton, Theophilus & Proctor, James Toyne	1842-57	48 Waterside South
Chambers, James	1822-35	Phoenix Foundry, Waterside South
Clarke, Edward	1859-75	3 Hungate, 1859-c.71; Coultham Street, from c. 1871 Known as Patent Crank Works, 1872 onwards
Clarke's Crank Co. Ltd	1875-85	Coultham Street
Clarke's Crank & Forge Co. Ltd	1885-2003	Coultham Street (now Kesteven Street)
Clayton & Shuttleworth	1842-1936	Stamp End Works, Waterside South, Electric power station, Spa Road, 1914 (Sold to Lincoln Corporation, 1917). Titanic Works (1912 to 1920). Abbey Works (1916 to 1920). Clayton Forge (1916 to 1920). Tower Works (opened in 1916)
Clayton Wagons	1920-30	Titanic Works, Abbey Works and Clayton Forge
Clayton Dewandre	1928	Titanic Works
Cooke, John	1852-1938	Eagle, near Lincoln, 1852-58
Lindum Plough Works	1858-c.71.	Monks Road/Rosemary Lane
Lindum Plough Works	c.1871-1938	Monks Road/Montague Street (opposite Cattle Market)
Copeland, Thomas	c.1812-14	Phoenix Foundry, St Swithin's parish
Dixon, Joseph & Thomas	1841-43	Swing Bridge, then 1 Broadgate
Dixon, Thomas	1842-43	13 Newland Street
Dixon, Joseph	1854-63	Broadgate & Pelham Street
Duckering, Richard & Burton, Edward	1845-55	Waterside South
Duckering, Richard	1855-70	Waterside North, from 1859

Name of firm	Dates	Location(s)[2]
Duckering, Charles	1870-1912	Waterside North; Monks Road showroom opened 1907 and closed 1966
Duckering, Richard & Co.	1912-62	Waterside North
Foster, William and Hartley, John	1845-48	Brayford Wharf East
Foster, William & Co.	1848-1960	Wellington Foundry, Waterside North, 1848- 1900. Woodworking site opened, New Boultham, 1885. Complete relocation to New Wellington Foundry, New Boultham, 1900
Fox, George Maples	1861-76	206/7 High Street
Hall, James & Co.	1870-75	Midland Iron Works, Brayford Wharf East
Harrison, Thomas	1861-86	Burton Road
Harrison, Teague & Birch	1876-83	Malleable Iron Works, Brayford Wharf East
Harrison & Co.	1883-1904	Malleable Iron Works, Brayford Wharf East
Harrison & Co. (Lincoln) Ltd	1904-32	Malleable Iron Works, Brayford Wharf East (1904-23). Also opened site at North Hykeham, 1905, to which fully relocated by 1923
Keep, George William	1881-1913	61 Portland Street & Reliance Iron Works, Cross Street
Key, John	c.1815-45	Broadgate
Lee, Joseph & Borland, Adam	c.1859	Norman Street
Lee, George	1896-1913	Wilson Street, Burton Road
Lyon, William Thomas	1922-30	73 Bailgate, then Drury Lane
Malam, John	1808	Waterside South
Malam, Rebecca & Joseph	1808-c.15	Waterside South
Malam, Joseph & Mumby, William	c.1815-20	Waterside South
Mitton, William	1842-61	City Wire Works, 25 The Strait
Mitton & Co.	1861-1963	16 Broadgate
Nicholson, Thomas	1842-57	5 Burton Road

Name of firm	Dates	Location(s)[2]
Oliver Brothers	1922-30	High Street
Pearson, Matthew	c.1900-c.34	Boultham Iron Works, Beevor Street/Waterloo Street
Penistan, Michael & Co.	1845-70	Broadgate, 1845-55; St Rumbold Street, 1855-70
Penney & Co. Ltd	1872-1919	6 Broadgate and City Iron & Wire Works, 1872-1961
Penney & Porter	1919-68	Outer Circle Road
Pool, William & Barrow	1832-56	Fish Hill/Michaelgate
Porter, J.T.B	c. 1860-1919	Gowts Bridge Works. Merged with Penney & Co. in 1919
Quipp, Henry	1881-93	Depot Street, Gas Street
Quipp, Walter	1913	Carholme Road
Rainforth, William & Sons	1869-1924	Britannia Iron Works, St Rumbold Street. Opened showroom on Monks Road, 1887. Manufacturing relocated to Foster's former Wellington Foundry, Waterside North, 1900
Rainforth, W. & Sons Ltd Co.	1924-54	Britannia Iron Works, Waterside North.
Revill, Charles	1834-89	High Street/Cornhill
Revill, Frank Clarke	1889-1914	Swanpool Court
Roberts, Joseph Henry	1876-93	3 Hungate
Robey, Robert & Watkinson, William	1854	St Rumbold Street
Robey, Robert & Scott, George	1854-57	Perseverance Works, St Rumbold Street; relocated to Perseverance Works, Canwick Road by 1856
Robey, Robert (& other partners)	1857-93	Perseverance Works, Canwick Road, renamed Globe Works in 1881, (trading as Robey & Co., 1857 onwards)
Robey & Co. Ltd	1893-1988	Globe Works, Canwick Road
Ruston, Proctor & Co.	1857-1918	Sheaf Iron Works, Waterside South, Sheaf Wood Works, Anchor Street, opened 1865. Boultham Works, opened 1916. Spike Island Works, Beevor Street, opened 1915

Name of firm	Dates	Location(s)[2]
Ruston & Hornsby Ltd	1918-61	Sheaf Iron Works, Waterside South. Sheaf Wood Works, Anchor Street. Boultham Works. Spike Island Works, Beevor Street (to 1930). Beevor Street Foundry, opened 1950
Ruston Bucyrus	1930-2001	Ruston Bucyrus jointly owned by Ruston & Hornsby and Bucyrus Erie from 1930. Occupied Spike Island Works, Beevor Street. In 1985, Ruston Bucyrus bought out by management, becoming 'R-B Lincoln' and then 'R-B International'. In 2000, company sold and 'RB Cranes Ltd' formed. Production ceased in Lincoln in 2001
Sawdon, Thomas	1793-1834	Swanpool Court, then Blyth's Yard, St Mary's Street, (by 1822)
Smith Clayton Forge	1929-66	Clayton Forge purchased in 1929; Abbey Works bought in 1935. Company sold to GKN in 1966
Taplin, Benjamin & Lee, Joseph	c. 1860-62	Patent Crank works, St Peter at Gowts parish (traded as Taplin & Co.)
Trotter, Theodore & Reuben	1861-69	204 High Street
Trotter, Reuben	1869-81	204 High Street
Tye, John	c.1829-53	Hungate
Tye, John, Jr	1853-70	St Mark's Iron Works, Brayford Wharf East

Notes

1. This information is partially based on a more extensive list of Lincolnshire implement makers which can be found in Ken Redmore, ed., *Ploughs, Chaff Cutters and Steam Engines*, (SLHA, 2007), pp.144-49.

2. Unless otherwise stated, the street names listed are those in use at the date of publication. Specific addresses, with street numbers, are those employed during the period of trading.

3. The majority of these details were obtained from company records, trade directories and local newspaper reports.

Bibliography

PRIMARY SOURCES:

Newspapers: *Lincolnshire Chronicle, Lincolnshire Echo, Stamford Mercury*

Trade directories: *Kelly's Directories of Lincolnshire, Morris & Company's Commercial Directory of Lincolnshire, Pigot's National Commercial Directories, Post Office Directories, Ruddock's Lincoln City Directories, White's Directories of Lincolnshire*

Significant archival and artefactual collections:

Clayton & Shuttleworth Archive (c.1845-1932), deposited at the Museum of English Rural Life, University of Reading

Media Archive for Central England (MACE), University of Lincoln

Museum of Lincolnshire Life, Burton Road, Lincoln

Robey Archive, Lincolnshire Archives

Ruston & Hornsby Project, Lincolnshire Archives

SECONDARY SOURCES:
Books:

Beastall, Tom W., *Agricultural Revolution in Lincolnshire*, History of Lincolnshire Committee, Lincoln, 1978

Brooks, Richard, *Lincolnshire Engines Worldwide*, Lincolnshire County Council, Lincoln, 1989

Brooks, Richard, Colsell, Lesley and Longden, Martin, *Lincolnshire Built Engines*, Lincolnshire County Council, Lincoln, 1986

Brown, Jonathan, *Steam on the Farm: A History of Agricultural Steam Engines, 1850 to 1950*, Crowood Press, Ramsbury, 2008

Clark, Ronald H., *Steam Engine Builders of Lincolnshire*, Goose and Son, Norwich, 1955. (reprinted by The Society for Lincolnshire History and Archaeology, 1998)

Clark, Ronald H., *The Development of the English Traction Engine*, Goose and Son, Norwich, 1960

Dewey, Peter, *'Iron Harvests of the Field': The Making of Farm Machinery in Britain Since 1800*, Carnegie, Lancaster, 2008

Elvin, Laurence, *Lincoln As It Was*, vols I-IV, Hendon Publishing, Nelson, 1974-81

Gurnham, Richard, *A History of Lincoln*, Phillimore, Chichester, 2009

Hill, Francis, *Medieval Lincoln*, Cambridge University Press, Cambridge, 1948

Hill, Francis, *Georgian Lincoln*, Cambridge University Press, Cambridge, 1966

Hill, Francis, *Victorian Lincoln*, Cambridge University Press, Cambridge, 1974

Hodson, Maurice, *Lincoln Then and Now*, vols I-III, North Hykeham, 1982-87

Jones, Michael J., *Roman Lincoln: Conquest, Colony and Capital (Revised Edition)*, The History Press, Stroud, 2011

Lane, Michael R., *The Story of the Wellington Foundry: A History of William Foster and Company*, Unicorn Press, London, 1997

Mills, Dennis, ed., *Twentieth Century Lincolnshire*, History of Lincolnshire Committee, Lincoln, 1989

Mills, Dennis, *Effluence and Influence: Public Health, Sewers and Politics in Lincoln, 1848-50*, Society for Lincolnshire History and Archaeology, Lincoln, 2015

Mills, Dennis and Wheeler, Robert C., eds, *Historic Town Plans of Lincoln, 1610-1920*, published for The Lincoln Record Society and The Survey of Lincoln by Boydell and Brewer, Woodbridge, 2004

Muir, Augustus, *75 Years: A Record of Progress: Smith's Stamping Works (Coventry) Ltd; Smith-Clayton Forge Ltd*, Lincoln, Ribble Road Works, Coventry, 1958

Neale, Andrew, *Ruston & Hornsby Diesel Locomotive Album*, Plateway Press, Gainsborough, 2014

Newman, Bernard, *One Hundred Years of Good Company. A History of Ruston and Hornsby*, Northumberland Press, Gateshead, 1957

Nurse, Pat, *'Devils Let Loose'. The Story of the Lincoln Riots of 1911*, Barny Books, Grantham, 2001

Pevsner, Nikolaus and Harris, John, *The Buildings of England: Lincolnshire. Second and Revised Edition*, (Antram, Nicholas, ed.), Yale University Press, Newhaven, 2002

Pullen, Richard, *The Landships of Lincoln. Second Edition*, Toucann Design and Print, Lincoln, 2017

Pullen, Stephen, *The Motor Makers of Lincolnshire*, Vols 1 & 2, Toucann Design and Print, Lincoln, 2007 and 2008

Redmore, Ken, ed., *Ploughs, Chaff Cutters and Steam Engines: Lincolnshire's Agricultural Implement Makers*, The Society for Lincolnshire History and Archaeology, Lincoln, 2007

Robinson, N.G., *Some Notes on the Steam Wagons of Clayton and Shuttleworth Ltd, Lincoln*, Newcastle-upon-Tyne, 1948

Robinson, Peter, *Lincoln's Excavators: The Ruston-Bucyrus Years, 1945-70*, Roundoak Publishing, East Nynehead, 2010

Ruddock, John G. and Pearson, Rodney E., *Clayton Wagons Ltd: Manufacturers of Railway Carriages and Wagons 1920-30*, J. Ruddock, Lincoln, 1989

Southworth, P.J.M., *Some Early Robey Steam Engines*, P.J.M. Southworth, Shirland, 1986

Stocker, David, ed., *The City By The Pool*, Oxbow Books, Oxford, 2003

Turner, John T., *'Nellie': The History of Churchill's Lincoln-Built Trenching Machine*, Occasional Papers in Lincolnshire History and Archaeology, 7, The Society for Lincolnshire History and Archaeology, Lincoln, 1988

Walls, John, *Ruston Aircraft Production: A Souvenir of Ruston's 1000th Aeroplane*, Aero Litho Company, Lincoln, 1974

Walls, John and Parker, Charles, *Aircraft Made in Lincoln*, The Society for Lincolnshire History and Archaeology, Lincoln, 2000

Wright, Neil, *Lincolnshire Towns and Industry, 1700-1914*, History of Lincolnshire Committee, Lincoln, 1982

Wright, Neil, ed., *Lincolnshire's Industrial Heritage – A Guide*, Lincoln, 2004

Journal articles and book chapters:

Agnew, John, 'Steam engines for heavy haulage on common roads — early trials and early apprehensions: 1856–1861', *The International Journal for the History of Engineering and Technology*, Volume 87,1, 2017, pp.64-80

Basquill, Sara, 'The hidden secret of a First World War tank', *Lincolnshire Past and Present*, 101, Autumn 2015, pp.14-15

Basquill, Sara, 'An explosive discovery: Ruston Proctor ZLH locomotive', *Lincolnshire Past and Present*, 106, Winter 2016-17, pp. 16-17

Basquill, Sara, 'Was this Nathaniel Clayton's apprentice piece? *Lincolnshire Past and Present*, 109, Autumn, 2017, pp.14-15

Basquill, 'Rescuing a "damsel in distress": ["Sylvie", a Ruston Proctor and Company traction engine]', *Lincolnshire Past and Present*, 121, Autumn, 2020, pp.12-13

Beevers, Ros, 'The birth of the tank', *Lincolnshire Past and Present*, 101, Autumn 2015, p.16

Betteridge, S.J., 'Ruston and Proctor Boilerworks, Firth Road, Lincoln', *Lincolnshire History and Archaeology*, no. 20, 1985, pp.65-6

Birch, Neville, 'Clayton, Shuttleworth & Co. – early success and a strike', *Lincolnshire Past and Present*, 50, Winter 2002-03, pp.3-5

Birse, Ronald, 'Shuttleworth, Joseph (1819-1883)'. *Oxford Dictionary of National Biography*, Oxford University Press, Oxford, 2004

Brassley, Paul, 'Output and technical change in twentieth-century British agriculture', *Agricultural History Review*, vol. 48,1, 2000, pp.60-84

Broughton, Derek, 'He's gone to the foundry', in Walker, Andrew, ed., *Boultham and Swallowbeck: Lincoln's South-Western Suburbs*, The Survey of Lincoln, Lincoln, 2013, pp.18-23

Brown, Jonathan, 'Clayton, Nathaniel (1811-1890)'. *Oxford Dictionary of National Biography*, Oxford University Press, Oxford, 2004

Brown, Jonathan, 'Ruston, Joseph (1835-1897)'. *Oxford Dictionary of National Biography*, Oxford University Press, Oxford, 2004

Carle, Annabel, 'Jack Richardson and the Lincoln Motor Manufacturing Company', *Lincolnshire Past and Present*, 73, Autumn 2008, pp.8-13

Cartwright, Adam, 'Rainforth's of Lincoln', *Lincolnshire History and Archaeology*, no.45, 2010, pp.41-49

Cerrino, M., 'William Pool, inventor, whitesmith, bell hanger and wag', *The Journal of the Lincolnshire Family History Society*, Vol.19, 2008, pp.124-127

Clarke, Lesley, 'Swanpool Garden Suburb', in Walker, Andrew, ed., *Birchwood, Hartsholme and Swanpool: Lincoln's Outer South-Western Suburbs*, The Survey of Lincoln, 2014, pp.31-33

Cooke, Hugh, 'John Cooke & Sons of Lincoln: prize plough maker', in Redmore, Ken, ed., *Ploughs, Chaff Cutters and Steam Engines: Lincolnshire's Agricultural Implement Makers*, The Society for Lincolnshire History and Archaeology, Lincoln, 2007, pp.24-35

Dewey, Peter, 'The British agricultural machinery industry, 1914-1939: boom, crisis and response', *Agricultural History*, vol. 69,2, 1995, pp.298-313

Duckering, Mark, 'Richard Duckering of Lincoln: ironfounder', in Redmore, Ken, ed., *Ploughs, Chaff Cutters and Steam Engines: Lincolnshire's Agricultural Implement Makers*, The Society for Lincolnshire History and Archaeology, Lincoln, 2007, pp.46-55

Evans, Gwyn, 'A reappraisal of Lincoln tank production in 1916', *Lincolnshire History and Archaeology*, no.50, 2015, pp.95-105

Hanson, Frank, 'Urban renewal in the Monks Road district', in Walker, Andrew, ed., *Monks Road: Lincoln's East End Through Time*, The Survey of Lincoln, Lincoln, 2006, pp. 56-61

Herridge, John, 'Industrial archaeology in Wigford', in Hill, Peter, R., ed., *Wigford: Historic Lincoln South of the River*, The Survey of Lincoln, Lincoln, 2000, pp.24-25

Herridge, John, 'Industry', in Walker, Andrew, ed., *Monks Road: Lincoln's East End Through Time*, The Survey of Lincoln, Lincoln, 2006, pp.13-15

Hill, Francis, (revised by McConnell, Anita), 'Tritton, Sir William Ashbee (1875-1946)'. *Oxford Dictionary of National Biography*, Oxford University Press, Oxford, 2004

Hodson, Maurice, 'New Boultham', in Walker, Andrew, ed., *Boultham and Swallowbeck: Lincoln's South-Western Suburbs*, The Survey of Lincoln, Lincoln, 2013, pp.14-17

Johnson, Chris, 'Canwick Road and Robey's', in Walker, Andrew, ed., *South-East Lincoln: Canwick Road, South Common, St Catherine's and Bracebridge*, The Survey of Lincoln, Lincoln, 2011, pp.35-37

Knapp, Malcom G. (compiler), 'Industrial Archaeology Notes 1979'. *Lincolnshire History and Archaeology* 15, 1980, pp. 55-63

Lester, Chris, 'W.H. Chester, steam engine builder, Lincoln', *Lincolnshire Past and Present*, 2, Winter 1990-91, pp.14-15

Lester, Chris, 'Gwynne's pumps at Wiggenhall St Germans', *Lincolnshire Past and Present*, 83, Spring 2011, pp.10-11

Moore, Nicholas, 'Pictures from Budapest – Clayton and Shuttleworth in Europe', *Lincolnshire Past and Present*, 115, Spring 2019, pp.3-8

Page, Chris, 'Agricultural machinery making in upper Lincoln', in Walker, Andrew, ed., *Uphill Lincoln I: Burton Road, Newport, and the Ermine Estate*, The Survey of Lincoln, Lincoln, 2009, pp.39-42

Page, Chris, 'Thomas Sawdon, machine maker and Sawdon's Yard', in Walker, Andrew, ed., *Brayford Pool: Lincoln's Waterfront Through Time*, The Survey of Lincoln, Lincoln, 2012, pp. 19-23

Page, Chris, 'A history of Michael Penistan Jr, agricultural engineer, Lincoln', *Lincolnshire History and Archaeology*, no.49, 2014, pp.9-22

Page, Chris, 'Mills in the parish of St Peter-at-Gowts', in Walker, Andrew, ed., *Lincoln's City Centre South of the River Witham: From High Bridge to South Park*, The Survey of Lincoln, Lincoln, 2016, pp.41-43

Parker, Charles, 'World War I hangars at Bracebridge Heath, Lincoln', *Lincolnshire Past and Present*, 48, Summer 2002, pp.14-15

Parker, Charles, 'Ruston Proctor Steam Navvy No. 306', *Lincolnshire Past and Present*, 110, Winter 2017-18, pp.26-27

Smith, Colin, 'West End high-tech industry', in Walker, Andrew, ed., *Lincoln's West End: A History*, The Survey of Lincoln, Lincoln, 2008, pp.28-31

Smith, Miriam, 'The growth and decline of the manufacturing firm of Clayton and Shuttleworth', in Walker, Andrew, ed., *South-East Lincoln: Canwick Road, South Common, St Catherine's and Bracebridge*, The Survey of Lincoln, Lincoln, 2011, pp.38-41

Stevenson, Peter, 'In the land of the giants: the 1957 Ruston Bucyrus export sales conference', *Lincolnshire Past and Present*, 98, Winter 2014-15, pp.17-20

Tate, Norman, 'The Malleable, North Hykeham: castings for agriculture and the motor industry', in Redmore, Ken, ed., *Ploughs, Chaff Cutters and Steam Engines: Lincolnshire's Agricultural Implement Makers*, The Society for Lincolnshire History and Archaeology, Lincoln, 2007, pp.103-111

Wheeler, Rob, 'From steam packets to Vienna: a new perspective on Clayton and Shuttleworth', *Lincoln Enquirer*, 21, November 2011, pp.8-10

Wheeler, Rob, 'The rise of Clayton and Shuttleworth', *Lincolnshire History and Archaeology*, no.47, 2012, pp.59-69

Wheeler, Rob, 'The decline and fall of Clayton and Shuttleworth. Part 1: The view from the sales office', *Lincolnshire Past and Present*, 89, Autumn 2012, p.4-7

Wheeler, Rob, 'The decline and fall of Clayton and Shuttleworth. Part 2: Innovation abroad', *Lincolnshire Past and Present*, 90, Winter 2012-13, p.8

Williams, John, 'The Shuttleworth family of Lincoln and Old Warden' *Lincolnshire Past and Present*, 52, Summer 2003, pp.16-18

Wilson, Catherine, 'Lincoln: street furniture of Motherby Hill', *Lincolnshire History and Archaeology*, no.15, 1980, pp.57-60

Wilson, Catherine, 'Stamp End Ironworks, Lincoln', *Lincolnshire History and Archaeology*, no.18, 1983, pp.116-17

Wright, Neil, 'The varied fortunes of heavy and manufacturing industry, 1914-87', in Mills, Dennis, ed., *Twentieth Century Lincolnshire*, History of Lincolnshire Committee, Lincoln, 1989, pp.74-102

Wright, Neil, 'Tour A: Lincoln (walking tour)', in Redmore, Ken, ed., *Lincolnshire's Industrial Past: A guide to 12 tours arranged by The Society for Lincolnshire History and Archaeology for the Annual Conference of the Association for Industrial Archaeology*, Lincoln, 2009, pp.5-8

Yeates-Langley, Ann, 'The West Common at war: Number Four Acceptance Park', in Walker, Andrew, ed., *Lincoln's West End: A History*, The Survey of Lincoln, Lincoln, 2008, pp.50-52

Yeates-Langley, Ann, 'Harrison's Malleable Iron Works', in Walker, Andrew, ed., *Brayford Pool: Lincoln's Waterfront Through Time*, The Survey of Lincoln, Lincoln, 2012, pp. 24-25

Yeates-Langley, Ann, 'Women munition workers in Lincoln during the First World War', *Lincolnshire History and Archaeology*, no.49, 2014, pp.129-138. (Originally published in the *East Midland Historian*, vol.7, 1997, pp.29-35)

Websites:

Arcade, Heritage Assets: https://arcade.lincoln.gov.uk/

British Newspaper Archive: https://www.britishnewspaperarchive.co.uk

Grace's Guide: https://www.gracesguide.co.uk

Heritage Connect: www.heritageconnectlincoln.com/lara-raz/heavy-engineering-works/724

It's about Lincoln and Lincolnshire: www.itsaboutlincoln.blogspot.com

Lincolnshire Film Archive, (www.lincsfilm.co.uk)

Lincs to the Past. The Ruston & Hornsby Project. Available from: https://www.lincstothepast.com/exhibitions/archives/the-ruston-and-hornsby-project/

Robey: https://robeyarchive.com/

The former Titanic Works, seen from Waterside South, September 2021. The building was constructed for Clayton & Shuttleworth in 1912. The company's initials are still evident in the brickwork at both ends of the building. (*Andrew Walker*).

Beevor Street, looking south east, November 1989. (*Jo and Steve Turner*).